THE PRINCETON REVIEW

McGraw-Hill Reading

TerraNova®
PREPARATION AND PRACTICE

Grade 1

Teacher's Annotated Edition

McGraw-Hill School Division

This booklet was written by The Princeton Review, the nation's leader in test preparation. The Princeton Review helps millions of students every year prepare for standardized assessments of all kinds. Through its association with McGraw-Hill, The Princeton Review offers the best way to help students excel on the TerraNova®.

The Princeton Review is not affiliated with Princeton University or Educational Testing Service. TerraNova® is a trademark of CTB/McGraw-Hill. This book has been neither authorized or endorsed by CTB/McGraw-Hill.

McGraw-Hill School Division ✍

A Division of The McGraw·Hill Companies

Copyright © McGraw-Hill School Division, a Division of the Educational and Professional Publishing Group of The McGraw-Hill Companies, Inc.

McGraw-Hill School Division
Two Penn Plaza
New York, New York 10121

Printed in the United States of America

ISBN 0-02-185718-0/1

3 4 5 6 7 8 9 066 04 03 02 01

CONTENTS

HOW TO USE THIS BOOK

Make Sure You Have the Right Level Book

The TerraNova test level your students take depends on what level TerraNova your test coordinator chose. Below are the test-makers guidelines, but check with your test coordinator to find out the exam level your students will take.

Level 10 Target Grade: Between the sixth month of kindergarten and the sixth month of first grade—usually kindergarten

Level 11 Target Grade: Between the sixth month of first grade and the sixth month of second grade—usually first grade

This Book Has Three Sections:

1. *The Student Introduction of Test-Taking Tips*

2. *Practice Exercises*

3. *Practice Test*

The Student Introduction of Test-Taking Tips

This section is four pages long.

What is the purpose of this section?

The test-taking tips included in the Student Edition give students basic information on how to take a test. Because test-taking is an unfamiliar experience for first graders, the tips included are important, fundamental suggestions.

How can I use this section in my classroom?

Review this section in class with your students. Ask them to follow along with you as you read aloud. Allow the class a chance to look at the pictures that illustrate each test-taking tip. Encourage students to ask you any questions they might have.

Practice Exercises

The Practice Exercises cover the skills tested on the Reading/Language Arts sections of the TerraNova. There are thirty separate Practice Exercises in this book. Each exercise is four pages long.

Practice Exercises 1 through 20 focus on Reading skills; Practice Exercises 21 through 30 focus on Language Arts skills, including phonics. The phonics questions in Exercises 21 through 30 unfold in the same sequence as they do in your McGraw-Hill textbook. This allows students the opportunity to connect and enforce the skills they learn in class with those that are tested on the TerraNova.

Some passages in the Level 11 TerraNova are student-read (read by the student) and others are teacher-read (read to the class by the teacher). Therefore, the Practice Exercises contain exercises with both teacher-read and student-read passages. In the Teacher's Edition, the Practice Exercises are formatted in two ways, depending on whether the passage is student-read or teacher-read:

- Practice Exercises that contain student-read passages are full-size, annotated student pages with answers and teaching tips provided in magenta.

- Practice Exercises that contain teacher-read passages are reduced in size and are accompanied by Teacher's Edition wrap, in which teacher script and directions are provided. Answers are marked on the reduced student pages in magenta.

In the teacher script, there are prompts to be read aloud. In order to provide the most realistic test preparation possible, read each prompt once. Then ask the students to fill in the circle that corresponds to the best answer choice. Read each prompt again before moving on to the next question. Always leave ample time for the class to fill in the answer circle.

What is the purpose of this section?

The Practice Exercises are formatted like questions on the real TerraNova. The students should use these exercises to familiarize themselves with the types of questions asked in the Reading/Language Arts section of the test.

How can I use this section in my classroom?

The Practice Exercises can be used in several different ways. It's up to you to decide which way is best.

- Complete the exercises throughout the year. There are thirty sets of Practice Exercises, one for each chapter in your McGraw-Hill textbook. After you finish a chapter, work through the associated exercise with your students.

- Complete one or two sets of exercises per day during the month before the TerraNova is to be administered. Do the exercises, then take fifteen minutes to review some general techniques that apply to that section and that help students with difficult questions. Always make sure that questions are addressed as soon as possible after reviewing the exercises.

Practice Test

The Practice Test included within this book contains questions that test the same skills that are covered in the actual Reading and Language Arts section of the TerraNova. Word Analysis, Spelling, Language Mechanics, and Vocabulary subtests are not included. If your students are taking the TerraNova this year, they will take the Complete Battery TerraNova since there is no Survey TerraNova for Level 11. The Complete Battery TerraNova consists of 45 Reading and Language Arts questions and should be administered in 1 hour.

What is the purpose of this section?

The Practice Test allows your students to experience what it would be like to take the actual TerraNova. In order to present your students with a realistic, simulated test-taking experience, administer this test to your students under the appropriate time constraints (1 hour) and circumstances (read the directions aloud for each section, ask students to remain quiet and seated throughout the test, do not give or allow students to ask for help) of a real Complete Battery TerraNova. Also, ask your test coordinator if students will be allowed to use scratch paper on the actual TerraNova. If so, make sure all students have scratch paper at the ready.

The Practice Test contains teacher-read passages only. Therefore, the Student Edition pages are reduced and annotated with the correct answers provided. Teacher's Edition wrap surrounds the Student Edition Practice Test pages and consists of teacher script and test directions. In the Teacher's Edition, the Student Diagnostic Chart and Class Diagnostic Chart are on pages T6-T8. Use the Diagnostic Charts to score your students' test and to determine their strengths and weaknesses.

How can I use this section in my classroom?

Although the Practice Test is at the end of the book, you might want to have students take it before or between the Practice Exercises. After they take the Practice Test, you can field students' general concerns and specific questions about the TerraNova, and then create your test-preparation plans accordingly. To help students absorb what they have learned, it might be helpful to allow for at least a day's rest between completing the book and their taking the actual TerraNova.

The Benefits of Using This Book

- Students become familiar with the "look and feel" of the TerraNova.

- Students learn systematic approaches to answering questions on the test.

- Students complete Practice Exercises to reinforce the test-taking tips they've learned.

- By completing this book, students gain a sense of accomplishment that helps them become more confident when taking the actual TerraNova.

- Students become more comfortable with "testing" environments and are less likely to develop test-related anxiety.

GUIDE TO THE TEACHER WRAP AND ANNOTATIONS

How the Annotations Work

The Student Introduction, Practice Exercises, and Practice Test sections of this book contain annotations for teachers. The annotations appear in magenta ink. In the Student Introduction, the annotations provide teachers with additional information students might need. In the Practice Exercises section, the annotations indicate the correct answer choice for each question in the Student Edition. In the Practice Test, the annotations indicate the correct answer choice for each question in the Student Edition, and also provide you with test-taking tips you might choose to pass on to your students.

How the Wrap Works

The teacher-read passages in the Practice Test and Practice Exercises are accompanied by teacher wrap. The teacher wrap contains teacher script, teacher directions, and the passage that teachers must read to students in order for them to answer the questions. In the Practice Test, the passage is on the left-hand page of the Teacher's Edition, and is not included in the Student Edition. The Student Edition pages that correspond to the passage are reduced and located on the right-hand page of the Teacher's Edition. Both teacher directions and teacher script are noted in the wrap alongside the Student Edition pages. Wrap that corresponds to a certain part of the Student Edition page is linked to the corresponding part of the Student Edition by an arrow. The wrap in the Practice Exercises is formatted similarly.

The diagram below illustrates the format of the wrap for the Practice Test:

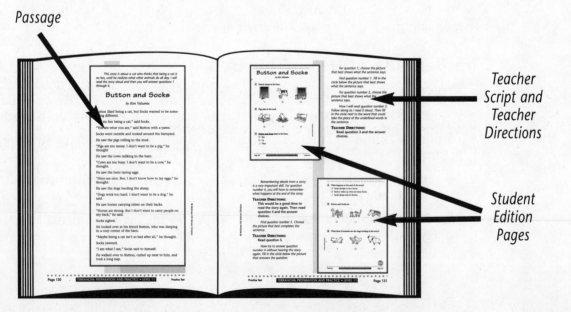

Passage

Teacher Script and Teacher Directions

Student Edition Pages

HOW TO USE THE DIAGNOSTIC CHARTS

The Class and Student Diagnostic Charts allow you to assess the strengths and weaknesses of your class as a whole, and of your students as individuals. Use these charts immediately after students have taken the Practice Test.

Student Diagnostic Chart

The two-page Student Diagnostic Chart allows you to assess students' skills and to see which specific questions present them with the most difficulty. Make enough photocopies of the chart so that you can assess each student individually.

How can I use this chart in my classroom?

Grade each student's Practice Test using the answers provided in the answer column. Please note that "First," "Second," and "Third" represent the first, second, and third answer choices, respectively. Each question is correlated with a question type. The unshaded box tells you which particular question type it is. When grading a student's Practice Test, put either an "I" (for "incorrect") or a "C" (for "correct") in the white box. After transferring the information from the Practice Test to each student's Diagnostic Chart, you can evaluate the question types that were most problematic for the student: First, add the total number of correct answers the student gave in each question type column. Then write that number in the numerator of the fraction at the bottom of the Student Diagnostic Chart in the row labeled "Total." The denominator tells you how many times each question type appears in the Practice Test. By placing the number of questions the student answered correctly in the numerator, you can specifically evaluate a student's strengths and weaknesses.

Consider using the Student Diagnostic Chart to show students where their strengths and weaknesses lie. If you think that students would be adversely affected by seeing a low score, the Student Diagnostic Chart might be most helpful as reference information in your students' personal files.

Class Diagnostic Chart

The one-page Class Diagnostic Chart allows teachers to assess their class's skills using the information gathered in the Student Diagnostic Chart. Photocopy the Class Diagnostic Chart if your class has more students than will fit on the page.

How can I use this chart in my classroom?

Write in each student's name on the left. Transfer the information held in the total row of each student's Student Diagnostic Chart. Then calculate each student's total Practice Test score in the last column of the Class Diagnostic Chart. After you have transferred the information contained in each of your student's Student Diagnostic Chart, you can assess the strengths and weaknesses of the class as a whole.

Question Types

The types of questions that most frequently appear on the TerraNova are listed in the Student and Class Diagnostic Charts. The question types found on the Level 11 TerraNova include: Main Idea, Specific Information, Drawing Conclusions, Vocabulary, Picture, Phonics, Paragraph Completion, Grammar, and Mechanics.

STUDENT DIAGNOSTIC CHART

QUESTION	ANSWER	Main Idea	Specific Information	Drawing Conclusions	Vocabulary	Picture	Phonics	Paragraph Completion	Grammar	Mechanics
		READING					LANGUAGE ARTS			
Button and Socks										
1	1st					X				
2	2nd					X				
3	3rd								X	
4	3rd		X							
5	2nd		X							
6	3rd		X							
Beach Clean-Up Day										
1	1st	X								
2	3rd							X		
3	3rd							X		
4	2nd				X					
5	1st					X				
6	1st		X							
Class Garden Story										
1	3rd		X							
2	2nd		X							
3	2nd		X							
4	2nd		X							
5	2nd	X								
6	3rd								X	
Trains Move Fast										
1	2nd		X							
2	2nd			X						
3	3rd			X						
4	2nd		X							
5	3rd				X					
6	2nd						X			
Aunt Betty's Farm										
1	3rd			X						
2	2nd	X								
3	1st								X	
4	3rd				X					
5	1st						X			
6	3rd						X			

STUDENT DIAGNOSTIC CHART

QUESTION	ANSWER	Main Idea	Specific Information	Drawing Conclusions	Vocabulary	Picture	Phonics	Paragraph Completion	Grammar	Mechanics
		READING					**LANGUAGE ARTS**			
Hopscotch										
1	2nd			X						
2	1st		X							
3	3rd								X	
4	3rd									X
5	3rd	X								
6	2nd		X							
Free Cat to a Good Home										
1	2nd								X	
2	1st									X
3	2nd		X							
4	3rd				X					
5	3rd						X			
6	2nd						X			
TOTAL	42	4	13	2	3	6	3	4	4	3

CLASS DIAGNOSTIC CHART

Student Name	Main Idea	Specific Information	Drawing Conclusions	Vocabulary	Picture	Phonics	Paragraph Completion	Grammar	Mechanics	Total
	READING					LANGUAGE ARTS				
	4	13	2	3	6	3	4	4	3	42
	4	13	2	3	6	3	4	4	3	42
	4	13	2	3	6	3	4	4	3	42
	4	13	2	3	6	3	4	4	3	42
	4	13	2	3	6	3	4	4	3	42
	4	13	2	3	6	3	4	4	3	42
	4	13	2	3	6	3	4	4	3	42
	4	13	2	3	6	3	4	4	3	42
	4	13	2	3	6	3	4	4	3	42
	4	13	2	3	6	3	4	4	3	42
	4	13	2	3	6	3	4	4	3	42
	4	13	2	3	6	3	4	4	3	42
	4	13	2	3	6	3	4	4	3	42
	4	13	2	3	6	3	4	4	3	42
	4	13	2	3	6	3	4	4	3	42
	4	13	2	3	6	3	4	4	3	42
	4	13	2	3	6	3	4	4	3	42
	4	13	2	3	6	3	4	4	3	42
	4	13	2	3	6	3	4	4	3	42
	4	13	2	3	6	3	4	4	3	42
	4	13	2	3	6	3	4	4	3	42
	4	13	2	3	6	3	4	4	3	42
	4	13	2	3	6	3	4	4	3	42
	4	13	2	3	6	3	4	4	3	42
	4	13	2	3	6	3	4	4	3	42
	4	13	2	3	6	3	4	4	3	42
	4	13	2	3	6	3	4	4	3	42
	4	13	2	3	6	3	4	4	3	42
	4	13	2	3	6	3	4	4	3	42
	4	13	2	3	6	3	4	4	3	42
	4	13	2	3	6	3	4	4	3	42
	4	13	2	3	6	3	4	4	3	42

AN OVERVIEW OF THE TERRANOVA

The TerraNova was developed to evaluate concepts, processes, and skills taught to students nationwide. There are four sections of the TerraNova: Reading/Language Arts (Reading and Language Arts scores are reported individually), Mathematics, Science, and Social Studies. There are also supplementary tests that support these core subjects: Word Analysis, Vocabulary, Language Mechanics, Spelling, and Mathematics Computation. If the TerraNova test your students will take contains such supplementary tests, "plus" will be added to the test name.

The TerraNova is offered in three versions: Survey, Battery, and Multiple Assessments, all of which have "plus" editions that contain supplementary tests as discussed in the previous paragraph. Check with the test administrator in your school to see which version of the test your children will take. Multiple Assessments is the only version that contains open-ended questions.

How Was the Reading/Language Arts Section of the TerraNova Developed?

The Reading/Language Arts section of the test was designed to reflect the new developments in education theory, while preserving the quality of past TerraNova tests. The people who developed the test worked with teachers, administrators, and other specialists in education. The test developers also consulted state curriculums, literature, and standards publications.

There are two major components of the test that are essential to evaluating children's skills in reading and language arts: the themes contained within the test, which provide children with meaning and purpose, and the classroom-like layout, in which children's major communication skills are tested.

The themes within each TerraNova test were developed to reflect the interests of the children, and are grade-level–appropriate. Each theme is introduced in order to stimulate the children's interest in the material that follows, and to direct their attention to the questions ahead.

Each of the reading passages that appears on the actual test was carefully selected. The passages are excerpted from well-respected traditional and contemporary literature. In order to create a heterogeneous scope representative of modern culture, the test presents various perspectives and backgrounds drawn from experiences common to North American children.

HOW SHOULD I INTRODUCE THE TERRANOVA TO MY STUDENTS?

Standardized tests are only an effective measure of your student's skills if they are administered properly. One of the best ways to make sure that the TerraNova is administered properly is to provide a good test-taking atmosphere for your students. The results of the TerraNova will be most indicative of your students' skills and knowledge if students are interested, motivated, confident, and clearly understand the directions provided on the test. To create the best test-taking atmosphere, consider the following guidelines:

1. Tell students why they are taking the TerraNova. Let them know that the test helps clarify what skills and knowledge they have learned and what skills and knowledge they have yet to learn. You might want to discuss the difference between a standardized test and a classroom test so that the students understand the importance of both kinds of tests.

2. Be positive about the test, both when you talk to students about it and when you administer it.

3. Encourage students to do their best. Tell them they cannot fail this test. Explain that some of the questions might ask them to use a skill they have not yet learned. Other questions might ask them to use skills they have mastered. Let the class know that they will encounter both situations, and that they are not expected to know all of the answers to every question. Also reinforce that this test in no way will affect their school grades. Encourage the students to:

   - answer each question, even if they are not certain of the best answer

   - read the directions carefully

   - use their time wisely and not get stuck on one question

   - review their answers if they have time when they finish their test

4. Foster the students' motivation by deciding not to use a reward system. Instead, help students understand the value of a standardized test. Explain that it is part of the learning process.

5. Pay special attention to the testing schedule and to the directions for administering the TerraNova. Organize your lessons in advance, and be sure to set aside enough class time for TerraNova preparation so that each section can be completed without interruptions. Students will be much more relaxed in an organized and controlled environment.

6. Familiarize students with the format of the particular version of the TerraNova they will take by exposing them to a similar testing format throughout the school year. Consider writing tests in a similar style. For example, if your students will take the Multiple Assessments version of the TerraNova, students should take tests throughout the year that contain open-ended and multiple-choice questions. This will make standardized testing procedures less unusual to students, and will ultimately facilitate a more positive experience when they take the actual TerraNova.

ADDITIONAL TEST-TAKING TIPS TO DISCUSS WITH YOUR STUDENTS

Consider discussing tests in general with your class. Regardless of whether or not your students will take a standardized test this year, they should start to learn important test-taking skills, such as:

- following directions
- developing good listening skills
- marking answer circles correctly

In addition to the test-taking tips supplied in the Student Edition, we suggest that your students also become familiar with less obvious test-taking skills. Some of these are noted below.

Taking Tests Can Be Fun

Discuss with students how tests can be fun if they are seen as:

- a chance to try out new knowledge
- a chance to show how much they are learning

Working Independently

Explain to students that during a test, they must do their own work. Students should know that:

- a test is not usually a group activity
- a test is designed to find out what each student knows by him or herself
- a test is nothing to fear—it is only one tool of many that you use as a teacher to make sure that your lessons are helping students to learn new skills

Being Quiet

Discuss the types of situations in which you expect your students to be quiet. Explain that test-taking is one time when students should be especially quiet. A quiet room during a test is important because:

- it's easier to hear the directions
- it's easier for them to think carefully about what they are doing
- the test is usually made to be given in a quiet room—it might not accurately measure your students' skills if the room is noisy.

WHAT SHOULD PARENTS OR GUARDIANS KNOW ABOUT THE TERRANOVA?

Since you and the parents or guardians of your students have the same goal—to help students do their best on standardized tests—make sure that they are informed about the TerraNova. Encourage parents or guardians to participate in the standardized testing process by helping to prepare their children for the test. Consider mailing a letter to your students' homes that discusses the TerraNova, the date it will be administered, the version of the TerraNova your class will take, the purpose of the test, and why the test is important. In your letter, you might want to include the following suggestions:

- Ask parents and guardians to encourage their children to use good study habits. Good study habits are useful in taking standardized tests and in class work, as well. Explain to them that good study habits include having a good mental attitude, following directions carefully, avoiding hasty errors, and reviewing their work.

- Let parents and guardians know the purpose of the test. Ask them to remind their children that the test is not something they can fail. The reason they are taking the test is to show the teacher what they have learned, and to show the teacher what they still need to learn.

- Ask parents and guardians to discuss with their children how being calm and confident can help them do their best on the test. Ask parents and guardians to explain that although the test is important, it is not something to be anxious about.

- Ask parents and guardians to make sure that their children get enough sleep and have nutritious meals every day. Explain that this is especially necessary prior to and on test-taking days, since taking a test requires a lot of energy.

- Ask parents and guardians to make sure their children arrive at school on time. Being late and rushing might cause the students unnecessary stress and could adversely affect how they perform on the test.

- Remind parents and guardians to ask their children about the test after it is over. Their concern and support is valuable, especially around the time the students are taking standardized tests.

© McGraw-Hill School Division

TEACHING STUDENTS HOW TO FILL IN CIRCLES ON THE ANSWER SHEET

In first grade, students are just beginning to hold writing instruments. For many, writing might still be an awkward task. Since the TerraNova is scored by a computer, it is crucial for students to learn the proper way to fill in the answer choice circles. If the students do not properly fill in the circle that corresponds to the answer choice they selected, their answer might be misidentified by the computer, resulting in inaccurate test scores.

Help students to understand the importance of filling in the circle completely. Tell them that a computer scores their test and that it will not "read" their answer choice if they do not fill in the entire circle.

The following page in the Teacher's Edition does not appear in the Student Edition. Consider photocopying it and distributing it to your students while you discuss the proper way for them to mark their answer choices. First, acquaint students with the test questions, answer choices, and circles. Show them where the question is, where the answers choices are, and where the circles are. Here are some important things to tell students:

- Make sure your pencil is sharpened before you take the test.

- Make sure you have an eraser on the end of your pencil.

- After you have selected an answer choice, fill in the correct circle completely.

- If you change your answer, erase the marks in your old answer choice circle completely. Then fill in the circle next to your new answer choice.

EXTRA ACTIVITY

To reinforce the task of filling in a circle completely, you might also want to consider doing some extra activities with your students. Help students practice filling in answer circles by having them practice filling in circles using crayons, markers, or pencils. Create a coloring sheet with balloons, flowers, a sun and moon, tennis rackets, and any other item you can think of that contains circles. Ask students to find the circles in the picture and then to fill them in completely.

MARKING YOUR ANSWERS

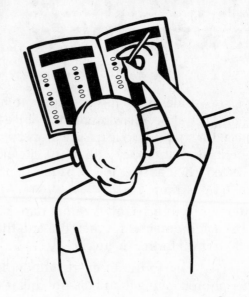

When you take the test, read the question and answer choices carefully. Then color the circle that goes with the answer choice you have selected.

Do NOT fill in half of the circle. This is wrong.

Do NOT place a checkmark over the circle. This is wrong.

Do NOT scribble inside the circle. This is wrong.

DO fill in the circle completely. This is correct!

Now, you try filling in the circle correctly.

On the test, how should you fill in the circle?

○ You should fill in half of the circle.

○ You should scribble inside the circle.

○ You should completely fill in the circle.

© McGraw-Hill School Division

LISTEN TO THE DIRECTIONS CAREFULLY.

Listen to all of the directions carefully. The directions tell you how to answer the type of question that comes next. Sometimes they even tell you the main idea of the passage that you will hear next. Always make sure you understand the directions before starting a new set of questions. When there are directions on your test page, make sure to read them carefully, too.

READ THE DIRECTIONS CAREFULLY.

READ THE QUESTIONS AND ANSWER CHOICES CAREFULLY.

Always read the *entire* question and *all* of the answer choices *carefully*. It is especially important to read all of the answer choices, even if you think one of the first choices is correct! Sometimes you will find a better answer.

GET RID OF THE WRONG ANSWER CHOICES FIRST.

Sometimes you will not be sure of the answer to a question right away. In these cases, you should always try to get rid of as many *wrong* answer choices as you can. Even if you can only rule out one wrong answer choice, you will have a better chance of guessing correctly.

DON'T SPEND TOO MUCH TIME ON ONE QUESTION.

The TerraNova is a timed test, so you have to use your time wisely. Try to answer as many of the questions as you can. You should still work carefully, though!

MAKE SURE YOU UNDERSTAND WHAT YOU ARE READING.

As you read the stories on the TerraNova, make sure that you understand what you are reading. Put the story in your own words.

Ask questions when you practice.

If you don't understand why an answer is wrong, ask me about it.

Do your best!

PRACTICE EXERCISES

Exercise 1

Say: Try this exercise on your own. Follow along as I read the directions.

TEACHER DIRECTIONS:
Read the directions, and then let students finish the exercise on their own.

Directions

Sheila has two younger sisters who are afraid of sleeping in the dark. Read "Bedtime for Sheila" and then answer Questions 1 through 7.

Bedtime for Sheila

Sheila had two little sisters.

They shared a bedroom.

Sheila liked to scare her sisters when they were in bed.

Q1 <u>"What is that noise in the closet?" Sheila said.</u>

"I see something moving under your bed!"

Her little sisters cried.

"You are such babies!"

Sheila laughed.

She thought it was very funny.

One day Sheila got her own room.

She felt grown up.

"Bye-bye babies," said Sheila.

"I have my own room now."

Q2 <u>"Good riddance," said her sisters.</u>

Q3 "We are happy."

Sheila did not care what they said.

Sheila was excited to sleep in her own room.

She climbed into her new bed.

Q4 She tried to go to sleep.

But she was scared.

The room was so dark.

And she was all alone.

Sheila thought she heard something under her bed.

She rolled over to look.

But there was nothing under her bed.

Sheila looked at her closet.

Was someone in her closet?

She opened the closet door.

But no one was inside.

She looked around her room.

She saw her pretty pink sheets

and her stuffed animals.

"There is nothing to be scared of in here,"

she said to herself.

"I love my new room."

Sheila went to her desk

and wrote a note to her sisters.

Go On

It said,

"I am sorry. Love, Sheila."

She slid the note under her sisters' door.

Then Sheila climbed back into her new bed

and went right to sleep.

1 How did Sheila scare her little sisters?

- ● She pretended to hear noises in the closet.
- ○ She dressed up like a gorilla.
- ○ She turned off the lights and hid under the bed.

2 Sheila's sisters say "Good riddance" when she leaves. What does good riddance mean almost the same thing as?

- ○ We will miss you.
- ● We are glad to see you go.
- ○ Please do not go.

3 Why were Sheila's sisters happy she was getting her own room?

- ○ Sheila's sisters are mean.
- ● Sheila will not scare them anymore.
- ○ Sheila will have pretty pink sheets on her bed.

Go On ⟹

4 What happened when Sheila tried to go to sleep in her new room?

○ She wanted to scare her sisters again.

○ She went right to sleep.

● She was too scared to go to sleep.

5 Why did Sheila write the note to her sisters?

● Sheila knew how bad it felt to be scared.

○ Sheila was sorry they did not get their own room.

○ Sheila was trying to scare her sisters again.

6 What will Sheila probably do the next time she wants to scare someone?

○ She will make the person cry and then laugh.

● She will remember when she was scared.

○ She will pretend she hears a noise in the closet.

7 Sheila sits on the bench.

○   ○   ●

Remind students to read the entire question and all of the answer choices before making their selection.

Exercise 2

Say: Try this exercise on your own. Follow along as I read the directions.
TEACHER DIRECTIONS:
Read the directions, and then let students finish the exercise on their own.

Directions

Tico and Mel want to have a contest. The one with the best snowman wins. Read the story and then answer Questions 1 through 5.

Tico and Mel ran out into the snow.

"Let's make a snowman!" said Mel.

Q1 "No. That is no fun. How about we each make a snowman?

Then we will pick the best one," said Tico.

"Yeah. One of us will be the best snowman maker in the world," said Mel.

"Number one," said Tico.

"The one and only best snowman maker," said Mel.

Tico rolled a big snowball for the bottom.

Mel did the same thing.

Tico rolled a smaller snowball for the top.

Mel did the same thing.

Tico tried to lift the smaller snowball on top of the big snowball.

Q3 But the smaller snowball fell apart.

Mel tried to lift his smaller snowball on top of his big snowball.

But the smaller snowball was too heavy for him to pick up by himself.

"How is your snowman?" asked Tico.

"Not so good," said Mel. "How is yours?"

"Bad," said Tico.

The boys were quiet for a minute.

Then Tico said, "You want me to help you pick up that snowball?"

"Sure! What about yours?" said Mel.

"We can use my snowball to make the head!" said Tico.

The boys worked together.

They built one amazing snowman.

Q4 Tico and Mel cheered, "We are the best snowman makers in the world!"

1 **Why did Tico and Mel start building two separate snowmen?**

- ● They were having a contest.
- ○ They wanted to make a snowman family.
- ○ They did not like each other.

Go On

2 Why did Tico and Mel think that a contest would make building a snowman more fun?

○ Working alone is easier.

● Having only one winner is exciting.

○ Tico's brother said it was more fun to have a contest.

3 What problem did both Tico and Mel have building their snowmen?

○ They did not know what to build.

○ There was not enough snow to make a snowball.

● They could not lift the snowballs alone.

4 What happened at the end of the story?

○ Only Tico was the best snowman maker.

● Tico and Mel were both winners.

○ Only Mel was the best snowman maker.

5 The best name for this story is

○ How to Make a Snowman Alone

○ Why It Snows

● Tico and Mel Make the Best Snowman

Remind students to get rid of as many wrong answer choices as they can. Even if they only rule out one wrong answer, they will have a better chance of guessing correctly.

Directions

For Questions 6 and 7, find the word that best fits in each blank.

Tico woke up and saw ____6____ on the ground. He was ____7____ because he wanted to go sledding.

6
- ○ rain
- ● snow
- ○ flowers

7
- ○ bored
- ○ tired
- ● happy

8 Tico and Mel go ice skating.

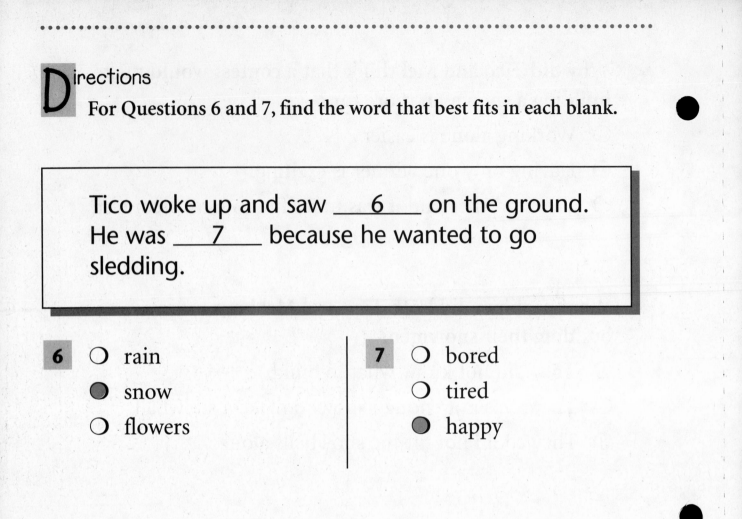

●   ○   ○

© McGraw-Hill School Division

Exercise 3

Say: Try this exercise on your own. Follow along as I read the directions.

TEACHER DIRECTIONS:
Read the directions, and then let students finish the exercise on their own.

Directions

Kia wants to get her mother something special for Mother's Day. Read the story and answer Questions 1 through 6.

Mother's day is tomorrow.

Q1 Kia wants to get her mother something nice.

Kia opens her piggybank

and counts her money.

Then she goes to the store

with her big brother.

Kia checks out perfume.

Kia asks,

"How much does this cost?"

Q2 She does not have enough money

to buy the perfume.

Next Kia and her brother go

to the flower store.

She asks,

"How much are these flowers?"

Kia does not have enough money

to buy the flowers.

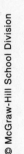

"I give up!" cries Kia.

"I do not have enough money

to show Mommy

how special she is to me."

On Mother's Day

Kia hangs her head low.

And she walks into her mother's room.

She gives her mother a drawing.

"Kia, I love this drawing!"

cries her mother.

Kia says, "I am sorry it did not come from a store."

"Oh Kia!" says her mother.

Q3 "It is more special to me

because it did not come from a store."

Kia hugs her mother and shouts,

"Happy Mother's Day!"

1 **Why did Kia go shopping?**
- ○ She needed a new shirt.
- ● She wanted to buy her mother a gift.
- ○ Her brother needed help picking out a gift.

2 Why didn't Kia get perfume for her mother?

○ It cost too much money.

○ She did not like the way it smelled.

○ The store was closed.

3 Why was the drawing so special to Kia's mother?

○ Kia paid a lot of money for it.

○ Kia's mother liked perfume.

● Kia made it for her.

4 The next time Kia wants to show her mother how special she is, Kia probably will

○ spend a lot of money on a gift for her mother

● make a gift for her mother

○ not give her mother anything

5 The best name for this story is

○ Kia Draws a Picture

● A Special Gift

○ Father's Day

Remind students to listen carefully to the directions. Sometimes the directions tell them the main idea of the passage.

6 Kia paints a flower.

      ○   ○   ●

Directions

For Questions 7 and 8, find the word that fits best in each blank.

> Kia and her brother stood on the ___7___ .
> They looked into the ___8___ and saw many fish.

7　● bridge

　　○ table

　　○ stage

8　○ room

　　○ book

　　● stream

Exercise 4

Say: Try this exercise on your own. Follow along as I read the directions.
TEACHER DIRECTIONS:
Read the directions, and then let students finish the exercise on their own.

Directions

Tom has a part in the school play. It makes him nervous. Read what happened when he goes up on stage, and then answer Questions 1 through 7.

Q1

Q4 Tom's hands sweat.

Q2 He is very nervous.

He hears all of the people on the other side of the curtain.

He thinks about his lines.

Q3 He cannot remember the first one!

Q4 His heart pounds.

The curtain goes up!

He walks out on stage.

He looks at his mother in her seat.

Q6 She smiles.

Then Tom remembers the line!

Everyone claps when he is done.

Q5 Tom knows he was good.

© McGraw-Hill School Division

Go On ➡

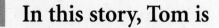

1 **In this story, Tom is**

⬤ acting in a play

◯ watching a movie

◯ eating dinner with his mother

2 **At the beginning of the story, Tom is very <u>nervous</u>. Which word means almost the same thing as <u>nervous</u>?**

◯ happy

⬤ scared

◯ tired

3 **What does Tom forget?**

◯ Tom forgets where to go on stage.

◯ Tom forgets to call his mother.

⬤ Tom forgets his first line.

© McGraw-Hill School Division

4 **What is something that does NOT happen before Tom walks out on stage?**

- ○ Tom's hands sweat.
- ○ Tom's heart pounds.
- ● Tom remembers the line.

5 **How did Tom feel at the end of the story?**

- ○ nervous
- ● proud
- ○ sad

Go On

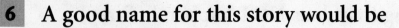

6 **A good name for this story would be**

⬤ A Helping Smile

○ Tom's Hands

○ Tom's Heart Pounds

7 **Tom eats ice cream.**

⬤   ○   ○

"Leaf Pile"

by Jonathan Yarkony

I raked them all into a pile,

orange, red, and yellow.

I stacked them high in the middle

And spread them out below.

I gathered them from my backyard

And from the neighbors' too.

Then I took a running jump,

And into the pile I flew.

Say: *This poem is called "Leaf Pile." It is about a boy playing in a pile of leaves. Listen carefully as I read it aloud to you. Then answer questions 1 through 14.*

Say: *Now I am going to ask you some questions about the poem. Then fill in the circle that is near the best answer choice.*

Say: *Look at the answer choices for question 1. Which picture shows what the boy made for himself?*

Say: *The next two questions ask you to remember details from the poem I just read to you. After I read the question aloud, fill in the circle next to the best answer to the question.*

Say: *Look at the answer choices for question 2. Why did the boy make the leaf pile?*

TEACHER DIRECTIONS:
Read the answer choices.

Say: *Look at the answer choices for question 3. Where did the boy find leaves?*

TEACHER DIRECTIONS:
Read the answer choices.

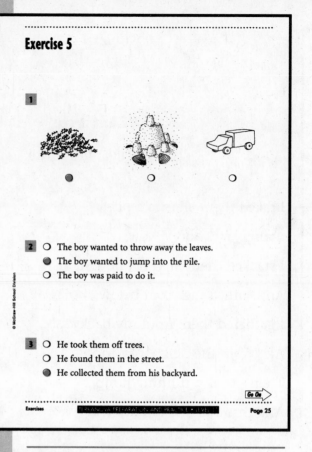

Exercise 5

1

2
- ○ The boy wanted to throw away the leaves.
- ● The boy wanted to jump into the pile.
- ○ The boy was paid to do it.

3
- ○ He took them off trees.
- ○ He found them in the street.
- ● He collected them from his backyard.

Go On

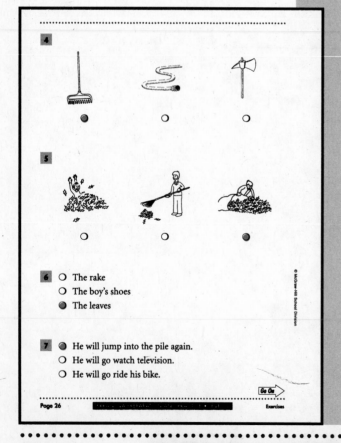

4

5

6
- ○ The rake
- ○ The boy's shoes
- ● The leaves

7
- ● He will jump into the pile again.
- ○ He will go watch television.
- ○ He will go ride his bike.

Go On

Say: *For the next two questions, fill in the circle under the picture that best answers the question.*

Say: *Look at the answer choices for question 4. What did the boy use to make the pile?*

Say: *Look at the answer choices for question 5. Which picture shows something the boy did NOT do? Make sure you pick an answer choice that is something the boy did NOT do.*

Say: *Look at the answer choices for question 6. In the poem, what are "orange, red, and yellow"?*

TEACHER DIRECTIONS:
Read the answer choices.

Say: *For question 7, use what you learned in the poem to choose the best answer. Look at the answer choices for question 7. What do you think the boy will do next?*

TEACHER DIRECTIONS:
Read the answer choices.

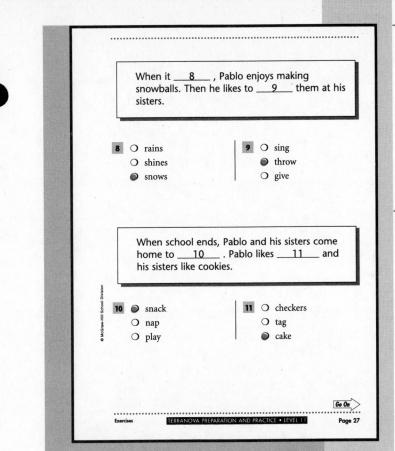

When it ___8___ , Pablo enjoys making snowballs. Then he likes to ___9___ them at his sisters.

8 ○ rains
   ○ shines
   ● snows

9 ○ sing
   ● throw
   ○ give

When school ends, Pablo and his sisters come home to ___10___ . Pablo likes ___11___ and his sisters like cookies.

10 ● snack
    ○ nap
    ○ play

11 ○ checkers
    ○ tag
    ● cake

Go On ⟶

Say: *For questions 8 through 9, choose the word that makes the best sense in the sentence.*

TEACHER DIRECTIONS:
Read the first sentence and the answer choices for question 8.

TEACHER DIRECTIONS:
Read the second sentence and the answer choices for question 9.

Say: *Now do the same thing for questions 10 through 11. Choose the word that makes the best sense in the sentence. Sometimes you might need to read the second sentence to know which answer to choose for the first question.*

TEACHER DIRECTIONS:
Read the first sentence and the answer choices for question 10.

TEACHER DIRECTIONS:
Read the second sentence and the answer choices for question 11.

Say: *For the last three questions, I will read you a sentence. Then you choose the picture that best shows what the sentence says.*

Say: *Find the answer choices for question 12. Listen as I read the sentence.* **See the airplane.**

Say: *Find the answer choices for question 13. Listen as I say the sentence.* **Kathy looks out the window.**

Say: *Look at the answer choices for question 14. Listen as I say the sentence.* **See Tim tie his shoes.**

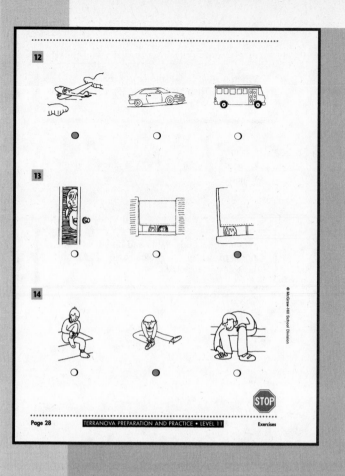

"Woodpecker Woes"

by J. Marlow York

I've been living in a wooden house
for most of my long days.
But recently, a friend stopped by,
moved in, and means to stay.

He's a downy woodpecker
with spots across his wings.
He taps, taps, taps around my place
and wakes me when he sings.

Each day his noisy tapping grows,
he never stops his pecking.
Louder than a hundred drums,
my hearing he is wrecking!

He's been with me for three weeks now.
My house looks like Swiss cheese.
I don't know why he just won't leave
and go back into his trees.

Say: "Woodpecker Woes" is the title of the poem I am about to read to you. A woodpecker is a bird with a long beak. It likes to knock its long beak onto wood. That's where it got its name. The word "woes" means troubles. Listen carefully as I read the poem. Then answer questions 1 through 14.

Say: Now I am going to ask you some questions about the poem you just heard. After I read the question aloud, fill in the circle near the answer choice that best answers the question.

Say: *Look at the answer choices for question 1. Who is the new roommate in this poem?*

Say: *Look at the answer choices for question 2. Which picture shows where the new roommate lives?*

Say: *Look at the answer choices for question 3. What do you think <u>tapping</u> means in the sentence, "Each day his noisy <u>tapping</u> grows, he never stops his pecking."*

TEACHER DIRECTIONS:
Read the answer choices.

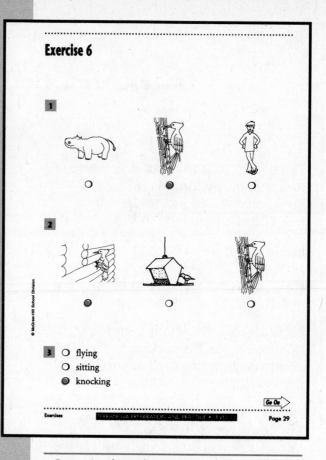

Exercise 6

3 ○ flying
   ○ sitting
   ● knocking

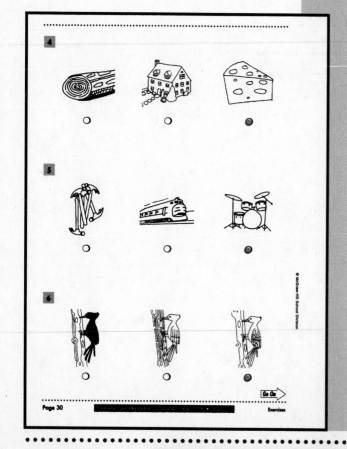

Say: *Look at the answer choices for question 4. What does the house look like after the woodpecker has been there? Use what you learned from the poem to figure out what the house looks like after the woodpecker has been there.*

Say: *Look at the answer choices for question 5. The woodpecker is described as being louder than what?*

Say: *Look at the answer choices for question 6. What does this woodpecker probably look like?*

7
- ● go away
- ○ go to sleep
- ○ eat dinner

8

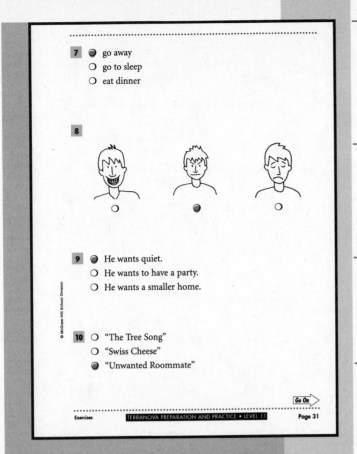

9
- ● He wants quiet.
- ○ He wants to have a party.
- ○ He wants a smaller home.

10
- ○ "The Tree Song"
- ○ "Swiss Cheese"
- ● "Unwanted Roommate"

© McGraw-Hill School Division

Go On ➡

Say: *Look at the answer choices for question 7. What does <u>leave</u> mean in the sentence, "I don't know why he just won't <u>leave</u> and go back into his trees."*

TEACHER DIRECTIONS:
Read the answer choices.

Say: *Questions 8 and 9 ask you to use what you learned from the poem to figure out which answer is the best. Look at the answer choices for question 8. Which picture shows how the person feels about the woodpecker?*

Say: *Look at the answer choices for question 9. Why does the person want the woodpecker to leave?*

TEACHER DIRECTIONS:
Read the answer choices.

Say: *Look at the answer choices for question 10. The name of this poem is "Woodpecker Woes." What other title would make a good name for it? Think about what the whole story is about.*

TEACHER DIRECTIONS:
Read the answer choices.

© McGraw-Hill School Division

Say: *For questions 11 and 12, find the word that best fits in each of the blanks.*

TEACHER DIRECTIONS:
Read the first sentence and the answer choices for question 11.

TEACHER DIRECTIONS:
Read the second sentence and the answer choices for question 12.

Say: *For questions 13 and 14, I will read you a sentence. Then you choose the picture that best shows what the sentence says.*

Say: *Find the answer choices for question 13. Listen as I say the sentence.* **Find the duck.**

Say: *Find the answer choices for question 14. Listen as I say the sentence.* **The teacher writes on the board.**

They had to stop the baseball game when the ___11___ went down. There were no lights to see the ___12___ .

11
○ moon
● sun
○ clouds

12
○ book
○ rocks
● ball

13

14

Exercise 7

Say: Try this exercise on your own. Follow along as I read the directions.
TEACHER DIRECTIONS:
Read the directions, and then let students finish the exercise on their own.

Directions

Darby Dog thinks Francie Fox is sick. But Francie Fox is not sick. Read the story and then answer Questions 1 through 6.

A Dog's Mistake

Q6,Q1 Darby Dog was going to the forest to see Francie Fox. He heard that Francie Fox wasn't feeling well lately. He was going to bring him some flowers. "These flowers will cheer Francie Fox up," Darby Dog said.

Q7,Q1 When Darby Dog got to Francie Fox's house, Francie Fox was outside jumping rope. "The flowers are very pretty," Fox said, "But I feel fine! SuSu Squirrel is the one who doesn't feel well."

Q2 "Oh my," said Darby Dog, "I feel so silly!"

"You shouldn't feel silly," Francie Fox said, "Everyone makes mistakes."

"Well, as long as I have these flowers," Darby Dog said, "we should go give them to SuSu Squirrel."

"That sounds like a great idea!" said Francie Fox. So they both went to visit SuSu Squirrel.

Go On

1 **Who was Darby Dog going to visit at first?**

   ○ SuSu Squirrel

   ● Francie Fox

   ○ Barry Bear

2 **Darby Dog says he feels <u>silly</u> when he finds out Francie isn't sick. What does <u>silly</u> probably mean?**

   ○ angry

   ○ happy

   ● foolish

3 **How will SuSu Squirrel probably feel when Darby and Francie give her flowers?**

   ○ smart

   ○ lonely

   ● cheered up

4 The story says that Francie Fox was jumping rope. Which picture shows what Francie was doing?

●   ○   ○

5 What title would be best for this story?

● "Flower Friends"

○ "SuSu Sings a Song"

○ "Darby's day at School"

6 Where is Darby Dog going in the beginning of the story?

○ Darby Dog is going home.

○ Darby Dog is going to the lake.

● Darby Dog is going to the forest.

Go On →

7 What does Francie Fox say to Darby Dog when he sees the flowers?

○ The flowers smell nice

● The flowers are very pretty

○ The flowers are small

8 Darby Dog should have guessed that Francie Fox wasn't sick. Why?

○ He was sleeping.

○ He had a cold.

● He was jumping rope.

Tell students that remembering details from a story is a very important skill. Remind students to look back at the passage if they cannot remember a detail.

© McGraw-Hill School Division

Exercise 8

Say: Try this exercise on your own. Follow along as I read the directions.
TEACHER DIRECTIONS:
Read the directions, and then let students finish the exercise on their own.

Directions

Dave and Tommy want to do something special for their mother. Read "Breakfast in Bed" to find out about the special thing they do for their mother. Then answer Questions 1 through 7.

Breakfast in Bed

Q3 "Come on, wake up," Dave said, gently shaking his little
Q1 brother, Tommy. "Today is Mom's birthday. Remember, we're going to make her breakfast in bed."

Tommy rolled out of bed and followed Dave downstairs to the kitchen.

"What are we going to make?" Tommy asked. "Can we make pancakes? Or eggs? Let's make waffles! I love waffles."

Q2 "You know we're not allowed to use the stove," Dave said. "We'll make a bowl of cereal."

Tommy found the biggest bowl in the kitchen. "Here, this is a good bowl," he said.

Dave laughed. "That bowl is almost as big as you are!" he said.

"Well, I want to make something special for Mom," Tommy
Q6 said, pouring an entire box of cereal into the bowl.

Go On →

Q4 Dave picked up the few pieces of cereal that fell on the floor. Then he took the milk from the fridge. He poured and poured, covering the giant bowl of cereal with milk.

Q4 He didn't spill a drop.

Q7 Dave put the bowl on a tray. He also put a glass of orange juice. "Ready?" he asked his little brother.

"Ready," Tommy said.

Q4 Dave lifted the tray and very carefully carried it up the stairs.

"Oh, wait a second!" Tommy whispered, "I have a card for Mom, too." Tommy ran into his bedroom and got the card he **Q7** had made. He put the card on the tray.

"Mom is going to love this," Dave said.

"Happy Birthday!" the boys shouted, opening the door to their mother's bedroom.

1 **What makes this morning special?**
- ● It is the mother's birthday.
- ○ Tommy is cooking.
- ○ Dave woke up early.

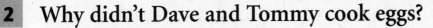

2 Why didn't Dave and Tommy cook eggs?

○ They don't know how.

○ Their mother doesn't like eggs.

● They're not allowed to use the stove.

3 What happened first in the story?

● Dave woke up Tommy.

○ Dave and Tommy sang "Happy Birthday."

○ Tommy went to sleep.

4 We can tell from the story that Dave is

○ mean

● careful

○ messy

5 This story is mostly about

● two brothers working together

○ kitchen safety

○ cooking breakfast

© McGraw-Hill School Division

6 The story tells us that Tommy pours an <u>entire</u> box of cereal into the bowl. <u>Entire</u> probably means

- ● all
- ○ none
- ○ a little bit

7 What does the tray look like that Dave and Tommy bring up to their mother?

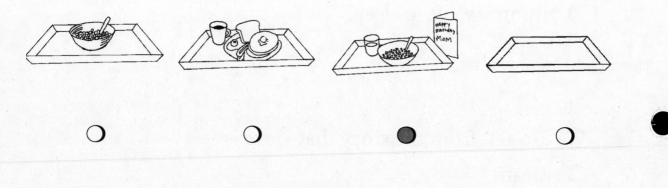

○   ○   ●   ○

> Remind students not to spend too much time on one question. Tell them to work carefully, but to try to answer as many questions as they can.

"Mommy, Teddy is sooooo . . . cute! He's light brown and furry. And you can pet him! I want one just like him!" Lola could not stop talking about her best friend Angela's new hamster.

"He's called Teddy because he's a Teddy Bear hamster. And he loves to run in his wheel. He runs forever in it!"

"I'm sure he is cute," said Lola's mother, "but I'll bet it takes a lot of time to care for him."

"Yeah. Angela has to make sure he always has food and water. And she has to clean his cage a lot. Yuck!" Angela wrinkled up her nose and made a face.

"Taking care of a pet is a big job. Are you sure you could handle it all?" asked Lola's mother.

"I can do it. I want my own hamster so bad," answered Lola.

"You're sure?" asked her mother.

"Yes! So can I get one?" cried Lola.

"Not so fast, young lady. Let's make a deal. You know that for a few days we are taking care of your uncle's dog, Buster?" said Lola's mother.

"Uh huh," replied Lola.

"I will give you the chance to show that you can take care of a pet. You can feed Buster and walk him. If you can take care of Buster, then we will get you a hamster. What do you think about that?"

Lola ran to her mother and gave her a big hug. "Thank you, Mommy! This will be great!" Lola was excited to show her mother how well she could take care of Buster. But taking care of a pet turned out to be a lot more difficult than Lola had thought.

Very early every morning, Buster would lick Lola's face to wake her up. She wanted to keep sleeping, but Buster wanted to go for a walk and eat. She had to get up to take care of him.

In the afternoons, Lola loved playing outside with her friends. But with Buster around, she had to stop playing early to walk Buster and give him his dinner. One afternoon, she stayed out playing too long. Lola found a big puddle inside the house next to the front door. She had made Buster wait too long and he had an accident in the house. So she had to clean it up AND feed him AND walk him!

"Whew!" Lola said to herself. "Taking care of a pet sure is a lot of work!"

A few days later, Lola's uncle returned from his trip and took Buster back home.

Lola's mother hugged Lola and said, "You did such a good job taking care of Buster! I'm so proud of you, Lola."

Lola was happy that her mother was proud.

"We need to go to the pet store and get you your new hamster! Have you thought of any names yet?" her mother asked.

Lola thought about it for a minute. "Mommy," she said. "Would it be okay if I didn't get a hamster after all?"

© McGraw-Hill School Division

Say: *Questions 1 through 3 ask you to remember details from the story.*

Say: *Find the answer choices for question 1. Which picture shows what kind of animal Teddy is?*

Say: *Find the answer choices for question 2. What did Lola tell her mother about Teddy?*

TEACHER DIRECTIONS:
Read the answer choices.

Say: *Find the answer choices for question 3. What did Lola's mother tell her about taking care of a pet?*

TEACHER DIRECTIONS:
Read the answer choices.

Exercise 9

1

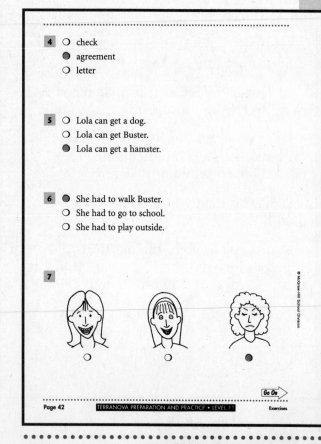

○   ○   ●

2 ○ I don't like the way he smells.
● I want one just like him.
○ I want to clean his cage.

3 ● It is a big job.
○ It is very easy.
○ It is always fun.

© McGraw-Hill School Division

Go On ⟩

---

4 ○ check
● agreement
○ letter

5 ○ Lola can get a dog.
○ Lola can get Buster.
● Lola can get a hamster.

6 ● She had to walk Buster.
○ She had to go to school.
○ She had to play outside.

7

○   ○   ●

© McGraw-Hill School Division

Go On ⟩

Say: *Find the answer choices for question 4. Lola's mother wanted to make a <u>deal</u> with Lola. Another word that means almost the same thing as <u>deal</u> is—*

TEACHER DIRECTIONS:
Read the answer choices.

Say: *Find the answer choices for question 5. Lola made a deal with her mother. The deal was if Lola could take care of Buster, then—*

TEACHER DIRECTIONS:
Read the answer choices.

Say: *Find the answer choices for question 6. Why did Lola have to get up early in the morning?*

TEACHER DIRECTIONS:
Read the answer choices.

Say: *Questions 7 through 11 ask you to use what you learned in the story to find the best answer.*

Say: *Find the answer choices for question 7. Which picture shows how Lola felt about coming in early from playing to take care of Buster?*

© McGraw-Hill School Division

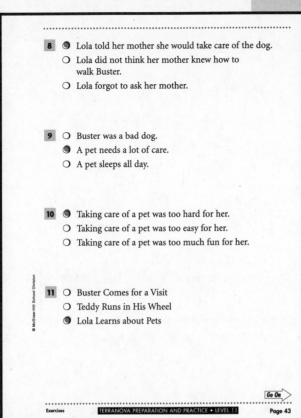

8
  ● Lola told her mother she would take care of the dog.
  ○ Lola did not think her mother knew how to walk Buster.
  ○ Lola forgot to ask her mother.

9
  ○ Buster was a bad dog.
  ● A pet needs a lot of care.
  ○ A pet sleeps all day.

10
  ● Taking care of a pet was too hard for her.
  ○ Taking care of a pet was too easy for her.
  ○ Taking care of a pet was too much fun for her.

11
  ○ Buster Comes for a Visit
  ○ Teddy Runs in His Wheel
  ● Lola Learns about Pets

© McGraw-Hill School Division

Go On →

Say: *Find the answer choices for question 8. If Lola wanted to stay out playing, why didn't she ask her mother to walk Buster?*

TEACHER DIRECTIONS:
Read the answer choices.

Say: *Find the answer choices for question 9. Why was taking care of Buster so difficult?*

TEACHER DIRECTIONS:
Read the answer choices.

Say: *Find the answer choices for question 10. Why did Lola decide not to get a hamster in the end?*

TEACHER DIRECTIONS:
Read the answer choices.

Say: *Find the answer choices for question 11. What would a good name for this story be? Think about what the whole story was about, not just parts of it.*

TEACHER DIRECTIONS:
Read the answer choices.

Say: *For questions 12 and 13, fill in the circle under the picture that best shows what the sentence says.*

Say: *Find the answer choices for question 12. Listen as I say the sentence.* **The girl walks the dog.**

Say: *Find the answer choices for question 13. Listen as I say the sentence.* **See Lola ride in the car.**

Say: *For questions 14 and 15, find the word that fits best in each blank. Sometimes you need to read the second sentence to know which answer to choose for the first question.*

TEACHER DIRECTIONS:
Read the first sentence and the answer choices for question 14.

TEACHER DIRECTIONS:
Read the second sentence and the answer choices for question 15.

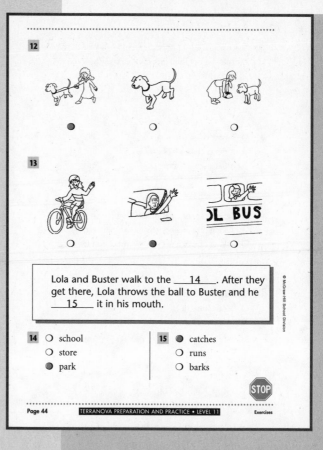

12

13

Lola and Buster walk to the ___14___. After they get there, Lola throws the ball to Buster and he ___15___ it in his mouth.

© McGraw-Hill School Division

14 ○ school
    ○ store
    ● park

15 ● catches
    ○ runs
    ○ barks

STOP

© McGraw-Hill School Division

"Kenny, recess is over!" called his teacher.

"Okay, Miss Rivera," said Kenny.

As Kenny stood up, he saw something under the slide. It was money! He picked it up. It was two dollars! Kenny stuffed the money into his pocket and ran to join the class.

Back in the classroom, the children sat down at their tables. Miss Rivera wrote some math problems on the board. "Try these," she said.

Kenny tried to do the problems. He had a hard time. All he could think about was the two dollars in his pocket. That was a lot of money! He thought about all the candy he could buy. Or he could buy a toy. Or some new crayons. He touched the money just to make sure it was still in his pocket. Yes! It was there!

Just then, Kenny heard someone crying. He looked around. It was Tina, sitting across from him. Miss Rivera heard it, too. She came over to their table.

"What's wrong, Tina?" asked Miss Rivera. "I lost my money," cried Tina.

Kenny felt sad for Tina. He did not like to see his friends cry.

"I'm so sorry, Tina," said Miss Rivera. "Have you looked in all the places it could be? Your backpack? Your coat?"

"Yes. I've looked everywhere. It's not there." Tina sounded miserable.

"Class," said Miss Rivera, "Tina needs our help. She lost her money."

All of the students were sad for Tina.

"How much money did you lose?" asked Miss Rivera.

"Two dollars," said Tina.

Kenny heard Tina. He realized that the money he found under the slide was Tina's money.

Miss Rivera said, "Class, look around you. Look under the tables. Tina lost two dollars. Let's help her find it."

Kenny did not want to tell Miss Rivera that he found Tina's money. So he pretended to look.

All of the students searched for Tina's money. No one found any money around the room or under the tables.

"I'm sorry, Tina." said Miss Rivera. "After school, you and I will go talk to the principal and see if anyone else found your money."

The class went back to their math problems. Kenny looked at Tina. She was still sobbing. He wanted to keep the money. But he did not like seeing Tina cry.

"What should I do?" thought Kenny.

He decided that he wanted to give back the money. He raised his hand. Miss Rivera came over. She asked, "Do you need help with a math problem?"

"No," answered Kenny. He pulled the two dollars from his pocket. "I found this outside by the slide."

Miss Rivera smiled at Kenny. "What a good boy you are, Kenny. Why don't you give it to Tina yourself."

Kenny got up and walked around the table to Tina. "Here, Tina. I found your money."

Tina stopped crying. She jumped up and hugged Kenny. "Thank you, Kenny!"

Everyone in the class clapped for Kenny. He felt proud. It was better than candy!

Say: *Questions 1 through 4 ask you to remember what happened in the story you just heard. Fill in the circle under the pictures that best answer the questions.*

Say: *Find the answer choices for question 1. What was Kenny doing when his teacher called him?*

Say: *Find the answer choices for question 2. What did Kenny find under the slide?*

Say: *Find the answer choices for question 3. What did Kenny do right away with the money he found under the slide?*

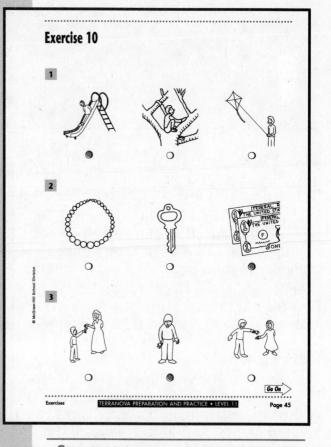

Say: *Find the answer choices for question 4. Which picture shows something Kenny did NOT think about buying with the money he found?*

Say: *Find the answer choices for question 5. When Tina told her teacher about her missing money, Tina sounded <u>miserable</u>. What does <u>miserable</u> mean?*

TEACHER DIRECTIONS:
Read the answer choices.

Say: *Find the answer choices for question 6. How much money did Tina lose?*

TEACHER DIRECTIONS:
Read the answer choices.

Say: *Find the answer choices for question 7. Why didn't Kenny want to tell his teacher that he found Tina's money?*

TEACHER DIRECTIONS:
Read the answer choices.

Say: *Find the answer choices for question 8. The story says Tina was sobbing. Which word means almost the same thing as sobbing?*

TEACHER DIRECTIONS:
Read the answer choices.

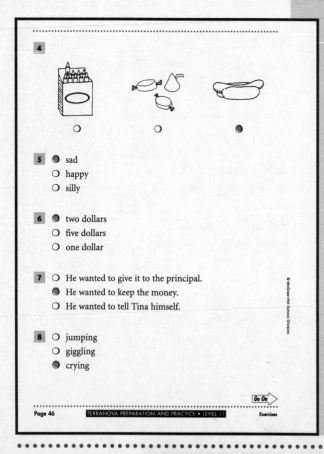

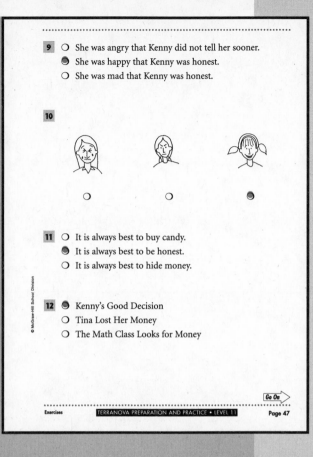

9. ○ She was angry that Kenny did not tell her sooner.
   ● She was happy that Kenny was honest.
   ○ She was mad that Kenny was honest.

10.

11. ○ It is always best to buy candy.
    ● It is always best to be honest.
    ○ It is always best to hide money.

12. ● Kenny's Good Decision
    ○ Tina Lost Her Money
    ○ The Math Class Looks for Money

© McGraw-Hill School Division

Go On →

Say: *Questions 9 through 12 ask you to use what you learned in the story to figure out the best answers. Think about the details of the story that might give you clues. Then fill in the circle next to the answer you choose.*

Say: *Find the answer choices for question 9. How did Miss Rivera feel when Kenny told her he found Tina's money?*

TEACHER DIRECTIONS:
Read the answer choices.

Say: *Find the answer choices for question 10. Which picture shows how Tina felt when Kenny gave back her money?*

Say: *Find the answer choices for question 11. What lesson did Kenny learn from this experience?*

TEACHER DIRECTIONS:
Read the answer choices.

Say: *Find the answer choices for question 12. What is the best title for the story?*

TEACHER DIRECTIONS:
Read the answer choices.

Say: *For the last two questions, I will read you a sentence. Then you choose the picture that best shows what the sentence says.*

Say: *Find the answer choices for question 13. Listen carefully as I say the sentence.* **The girl looks sad.**

Say: *Find the answer choices for question 14. Listen carefully as I say the sentence.* **Kenny looked under the table.**

Exercise 11

Say: Try this exercise on your own. Follow along as I read the directions.
TEACHER DIRECTIONS:
Read the directions, and then let students finish the exercise on their own.

Directions

Maria likes to run in races. Read about what happened this time when she ran in a race. Then answer Questions 1 through 5.

Q1 | Q2 | Q3

Maria knew she was last. She could see the finish line. It was far away. She did not want to keep going. Then she heard her friends cheering for her. It made her feel strong. She started to run faster. She was not stopping now. She wanted to win!

1 In this story, Maria is probably

○ dancing

◉ racing

○ acting

2 Why did Maria want to stop running at the beginning of the story?

○ She had a cramp in her leg.

○ Her friends asked her to stop.

◉ She had given up hope.

Go On

3 What happened when Maria heard her friends cheering for her?

○ She stopped running.

○ She wanted to give up.

● She ran faster.

4 The next time one of Maria's friends is struggling to do something, what will Maria probably do?

○ She will tell her friend to give up.

● She will tell her friend not to give up.

○ She will laugh at her friend.

5 A good name for this story would be

● Never Give Up

○ Maria

○ Winning the Race

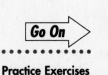

Directions

For Questions 6 and 7, find the word that best fits in each blank.

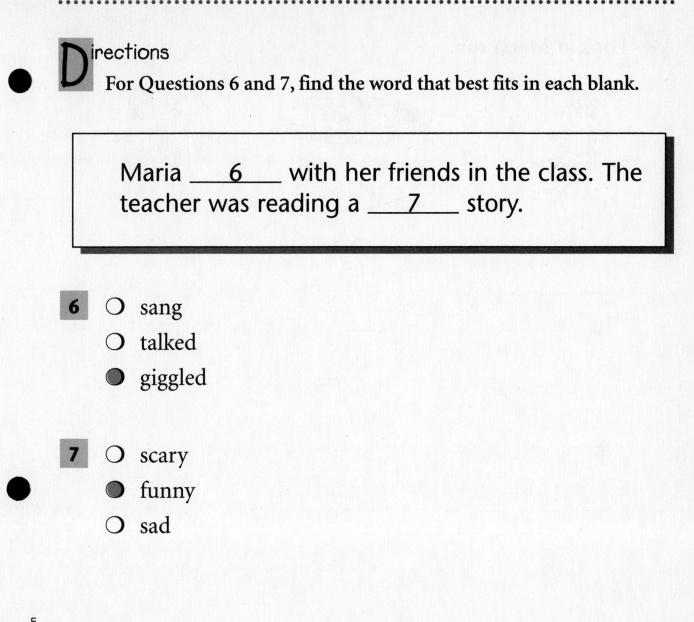

> Maria ___6___ with her friends in the class. The teacher was reading a ___7___ story.

6 ○ sang
   ○ talked
   ● giggled

7 ○ scary
   ● funny
   ○ sad

8 Look at Maria run.

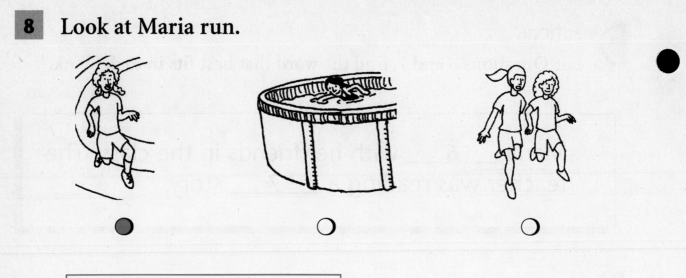

Remind students to get rid of the wrong
answer choices first.

"Free Time"

by James Yenta

My brother Jack plays basketball,
My sister Sue, ballet,
I like to sit and read a lot
At night or in the day.

My brother likes to shoot some hoops,
Sue dances like a queen,
I never need a class or ball,
Just a book or magazine.

Say: *The poem I am about to read to you is titled "Free Time." It's told by a child. The child tells you how he likes to spend his free time. Listen carefully as I read you the poem. Then answer questions 1 through 14.*

Say: *Questions 1 through 4 ask you to remember details from the poem you just heard. Listen carefully as I read the questions. Then fill in the circle under the picture that best answers the question.*

Say: *Find the answer choices for question 1. Which picture shows Jack's favorite game?*

Say: *Look at the answer choices for question 2. Find the picture that shows something Jack did NOT do in the poem.*

Say: *Find the answer choices for question 3. What does the child like to do in the poem?*

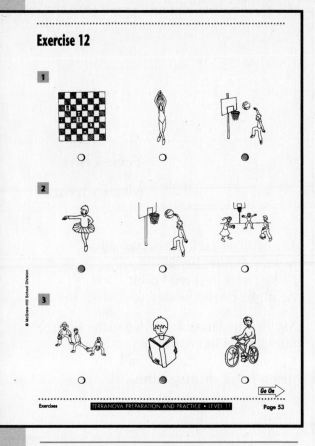

Exercise 12

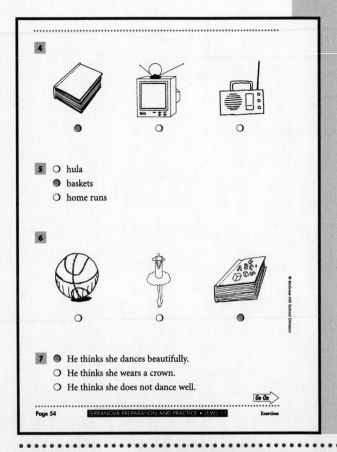

Say: *Find the answer choices for question 4. What does the child like to read?*

Say: *Find the answer choices for question 5. The poem says "My brother likes to shoot some <u>hoops</u>." Which word means about the same thing as <u>hoops</u> in this sentence?*

TEACHER DIRECTIONS:
Read the answer choices.

Say: *Find the answer choices for question 6. If you had to give the child who wrote this poem a present, what would you give him to make him very happy? To find the best answer, think about what you learned in the poem.*

Say: *Find the answer choices for question 7. The poem says "<u>my sister dances like a queen.</u>" Why does the child think this?*

TEACHER DIRECTIONS:
Read the answer choices.

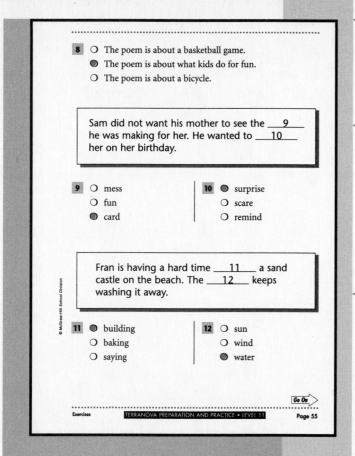

8 ○ The poem is about a basketball game.
   ● The poem is about what kids do for fun.
   ○ The poem is about a bicycle.

Sam did not want his mother to see the ___9___ he was making for her. He wanted to ___10___ her on her birthday.

9 ○ mess
   ○ fun
   ● card

10 ● surprise
   ○ scare
   ○ remind

Fran is having a hard time ___11___ a sand castle on the beach. The ___12___ keeps washing it away.

11 ● building
   ○ baking
   ○ saying

12 ○ sun
   ○ wind
   ● water

Go On →

© McGraw-Hill School Division

TEACHER DIRECTIONS:
Read the answer choices.

Say: *For questions 9 and 10, find the words that best fit in the blanks.*

TEACHER DIRECTIONS:
Read the first sentence and the answer choices for question 9.

TEACHER DIRECTIONS:
Read the second sentence and the answer choices for question 10.

Say: *For questions 11 and 12, find the words that best fit in the blanks.*

TEACHER DIRECTIONS:
Read the first sentence and the answer choices for question 11.

TEACHER DIRECTIONS:
Read the second sentence and the answer choices for question 12.

Say: *For the last two questions, I will read you a sentence. Then you choose the picture that best shows what the sentence says.*

Say: *Find the answer choices for question 13. Listen carefully as I say the sentence.* **See the tall building.**

Say: *Find the answer choices for question 14. Listen carefully as I say the sentence.* **Carla holds the baby.**

© McGraw-Hill School Division

"I Used to Be a Brand New Car"

by Jerome Yervane

I used to be a brand new car,
these days I'm not so fast.
A horse and carriage speed by me,
on freeways I always get passed.

My tires are bald,
my skin is specked with rust,
and all the new cars
leave me in their dust.

Say: *The poem I am about to read to you is about an old car. It is called "I Used to Be a Brand New Car." Listen carefully as I read the poem. Then answer questions 1 through 12.*

Say: *Find the answer choices for question 1. Find the picture that shows what the poem describes.*

Say: *Find the answer choices for question 2. What kind of car is described in the poem?*

TEACHER DIRECTIONS:
Read the answer choices.

Say: *Find the answer choices for question 3. The car says that, on freeways, it "always gets passed." What does it mean?*

TEACHER DIRECTIONS:
Read the answer choices.

Exercise 13

1

○   ●   ○

2 ○ the fastest car
○ a brand new car
● a not so fast car

3 ● It is moving very slowly.
○ It is moving very fast.
○ It is moving very quietly.

Go On

Say: *Find the answer choices for question 4. The car said he was slower than what?*

Say: *Find the answer choices for question 5. Which picture shows what the car looks like? Think about the details from the poem.*

Say: *Find the answer choices for question 6. Which picture shows a faster way for the owner to get to work? Fill in the circle under your answer.*

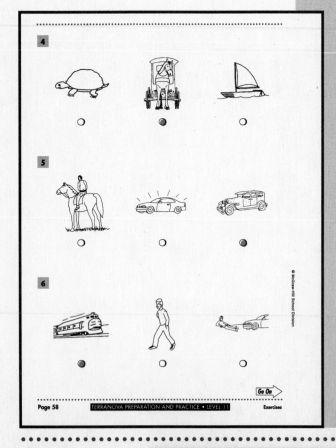

The car was out of gas so he stopped at a gas
____7____. The gas tank was ____8____ and needed
to be filled.

7 ● station
   ○ restaurant
   ○ parking lot

8 ○ full
   ● almost empty
   ○ heavy

By the afternoon, the driver ____9____ very hot.
The sun was ____10____ in the summer.

9 ○ smelled
   ○ tasted
   ● felt

10 ○ pretty
   ● strong
   ○ cool

© McGraw-Hill School Division

Go On ⇨

Exercises   TERRANOVA PREPARATION AND PRACTICE • LEVEL 11   Page 59

Say: *For questions 7 and 8, find the words that best fit in the blanks.*

TEACHER DIRECTIONS:
Read the first sentence and the answer choices for question 7.

TEACHER DIRECTIONS:
Read the second sentence and the answer choices for question 8.

Say: *For questions 9 and 10, find the words that best fit in the blanks.*

TEACHER DIRECTIONS:
Read the first sentence and the answer choices for question 9.

TEACHER DIRECTIONS:
Read the second sentence and the answer choices for question 10.

© McGraw-Hill School Division

Practice Exercises   TERRANOVA PREPARATION AND PRACTICE • LEVEL 11   **Page 59**

Say: *For the last two questions, I will read you a sentence. Then you choose the picture that best shows what the sentence says.*

Say: *Find the answer choices for question 11. Listen carefully as I say the sentence.* **See the boy milk the cow.**

Say: *Find the answer choices for question 12. Listen carefully as I say the sentence.* **The monkey hangs in the tree.**

Exercise 14

Say: Try this exercise on your own. Follow along as I read the directions.
TEACHER DIRECTIONS:
Read the directions, and then let students finish the exercise on their own.

Directions

Getting a new baby brother or sister doesn't always feel good. Sometimes it feels like your parents will treat you differently now that there is a new baby in the family. Read Diana's story. It tells how she felt when her new baby sister was born. Then answer Questions 1 through 8.

Q1 I got a new baby sister today. Her name is Regina. Regina
Q2 means queen. I am Diana. But my daddy calls me princess. Even though my name does not mean princess. I am special to him. He tells me so. I am scared that Regina will be more
Q3 special to my daddy than I am. But Daddy tells me he will
Q4 always love me. Even if there is a queen in the house now.

1 **What happened to Diana today?**

○ She got a new name.

○ She met her new baby brother.

● She became a big sister.

2 **Why did she say that there is now a queen in the house?**

● Her new baby sister's name means queen.

○ She decided to change her name from Diana to Queen.

○ Her daddy stopped calling her princess.

Go On ➡

3 In the beginning, how did Diana feel about Regina?

○ angry

● jealous

○ tired

4 Why did Diana's feelings about her sister change in the end?

○ She understood that her daddy could only love one daughter.

● She understood that her sister would not take away their daddy's love.

○ She understood that her sister wanted to be more special than she was.

5 The best name for this story is

● A Father's Love

○ Diana and Her New Sister

○ The Princess

Directions

For Questions 6 and 7, find the word that fits best in each blank.

Daddy took Princess and Regina to the ___6___.
They ___7___ elephants, lions, and bears.

6 ○ beach
   ● zoo
   ○ park

7 ○ asked
   ○ met
   ● saw

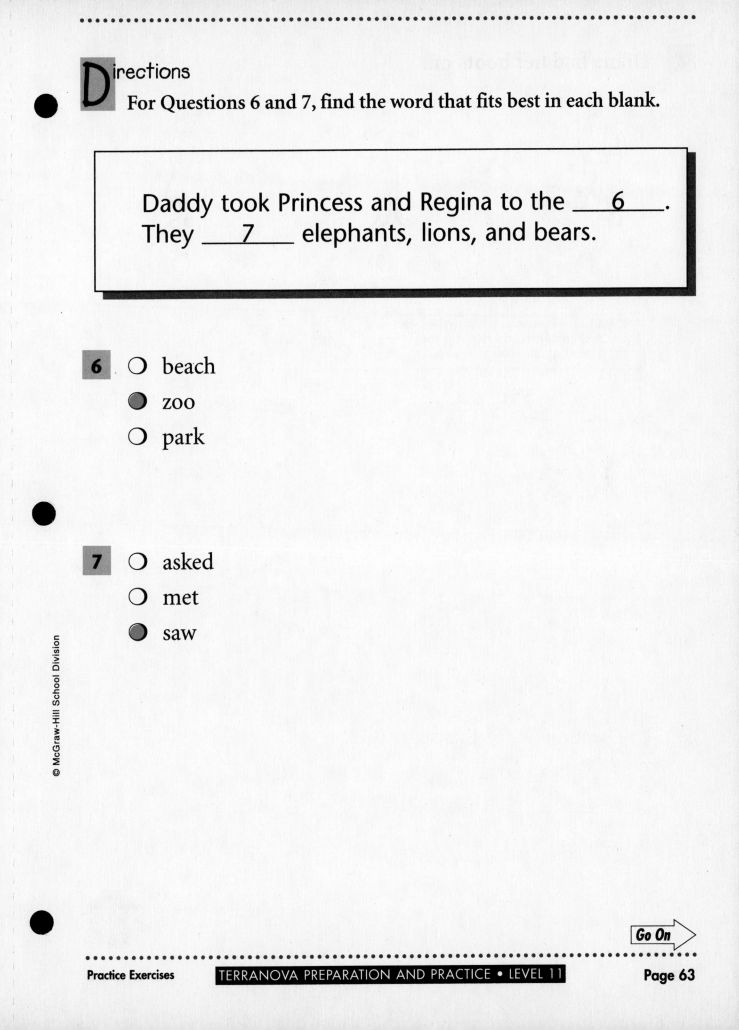

Go On

8 Diana had her boots on.

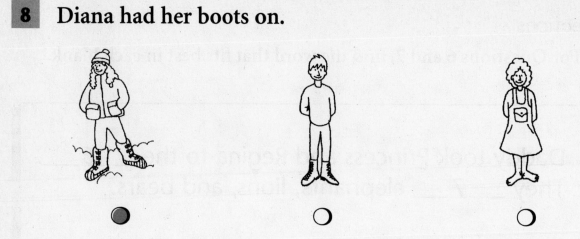

Remind students to read the directions carefully. Sometimes the directions can help them better understand the story they are about to read.

Exercise 15

Say: Try this exercise on your own. Follow along as I read the directions.

TEACHER DIRECTIONS:
Read the directions, and then let students finish the exercise on their own.

Directions

Read the story. It is called Maisy and Pug. Maisy is a cat and Pug is a dog. Then answer Questions 1 through 7.

Maisy and Pug

On Saturday George and his

sister Nina were sitting on their

back step, waiting to leave.

They were walking to a birthday party down the street.

Their cat, Maisy, was sprawled out

in between them.

"You cannot come to the party," George said.

Maisy licked her paw.

George and Nina stroked Maisy's fur.

Q3 | Maisy purred.

She was content to lay in the sun.

All of a sudden, it was time to go.

"Bye Maisy," George said, "We'll be back in a little while."

Maisy sat up.

She watched them leave.

Her tail twitched.

Go On ➡

Then, she started to follow them down the steps.

George looked back and saw what was happening.

"No Maisy, go back to our house," he said kindly but firmly.

But Maisy still followed them.

Q2 <u>When they got to the party,</u>

<u>George and Nina saw their friends.</u>

Then they saw Pug.

Q4 <u>Pug is a big dog that lives in the neighborhood.</u>

Oh no, thought George.

George, Nina, and Maisy stood together.

Pug watched them from the yard.

Maisy looked calm.

Q4 <u>"Go home Maisy," said George.</u>

Maisy stayed.

Pug growled.

Oh no, thought George.

Then Maisy did something funny.

She went over to Pug and licked him on the nose.

George and Nina sighed with relief.

They watched as Maisy and Pug ran through the grass.

Q5 <u>Maisy and Pug ran toward Mrs. Gregory's flower garden.</u>

<u>Oh no, thought George.</u>

© McGraw-Hill School Division

1 Which sentence best describes Maisy?

○ Maisy is a little cat who stays home.

○ Maisy is a big cat who growls a lot.

● Maisy is a happy, friendly cat.

2 Who did George and Nina see first at the party?

○ Pug

● their friends

○ their mother

3 Maisy was <u>content</u> to lay in the sun. Which word means almost the same thing as <u>content</u>?

● happy

○ sad

○ mad

4 Why did George tell Maisy to "go home" when he saw Pug?

○ He was worried that Pug would run away.

● He was worried that Pug would not like Maisy.

○ He knew Maisy and Pug were friends.

Go On

5 At the end, why did George think, "Oh no"?

- ● He knew Maisy and Pug would ruin Mrs. Gregory's flower garden.
- ○ He knew Maisy and Pug would get lost.
- ○ He wanted Maisy to go home.

6 The best name for this story is

- ● Maisy and Pug Are Friends
- ○ Why is Maisy So Lazy?
- ○ Pug is a Big Dog

7 Maisy and Pug ran through the grass.

○   ●   ○

Remind students to read the entire question and all of the answer choices, even if they think they know the right answer. Sometimes they will find a better answer choice if they keep reading.

Exercise 16

Say: Try this exercise on your own. Follow along as I read the directions.
TEACHER DIRECTIONS:
Read the directions, and then let students finish the exercise on their own.

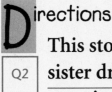irections

Q2 This story is called "Viv and I." It is about Viv and her sister. Viv's sister draws her a picture. Read the story. Then answer the questions.

Viv and I

"Please draw a picture for me,"

Viv said.

Q1 She knows I love to draw.

"Alright," I told her.

I took out my drawing pad and some pencils.

"All set?" Viv asked.

I smiled and said yes.

Viv began, "First make a square:

It is for the head."

I said, "A square for a head? Heads are not

square!"

Viv said, "This one is."

Q3 I said, "It's not right, Viv.

People have round heads.

You make a circle.

Then you draw the eyes, nose, and mouth.

Then you draw hair.

If you make the head square,

it will not look right."

"Just draw a square," Viv said.

"Okay," I said.

I drew a square.

Viv said, "Now draw two squares

for the eyes, one square for the nose and a

rectangle for the mouth."

I drew that.

"Anything else, Viv?" I asked.

"No, that's it," said Viv.

"Will you tell me what it is?" I asked.

Q4 Viv said, "It's a robot, not a person!"

"Great picture," I said.

"I know," said Viv.

© McGraw-Hill School Division

1 **Why didn't Viv draw her own picture?**

● She knows her sister loves to draw.

○ She was tired.

○ She could not find her sketchbook and pencils.

2 Who is drawing the picture for Viv?

- ○ a robot
- ● Viv's older sister
- ○ Viv's friend

3 Why doesn't Viv's sister want to draw a square for a head?

- ● It will not look right.
- ○ It will look too big on the paper.
- ○ Squares are hard to draw.

4 Why did Viv want the head to be square?

- ○ She wanted a picture of a house.
- ● She wanted a picture of a robot.
- ○ She wanted the picture to be different.

5 What is this story mostly about?

- ○ two sisters doing chores
- ○ Viv's dog
- ● two sisters making a picture

Go On

For Questions 6 and 7, find the word that fits best in each blank.

Viv likes to ___6___ in the woods. She likes to ___7___ in the fresh air.

6 ● walk
       ○ swim
       ○ sled

7 ○ sneeze
       ● breathe
       ○ cough

8 Viv wears a hat.

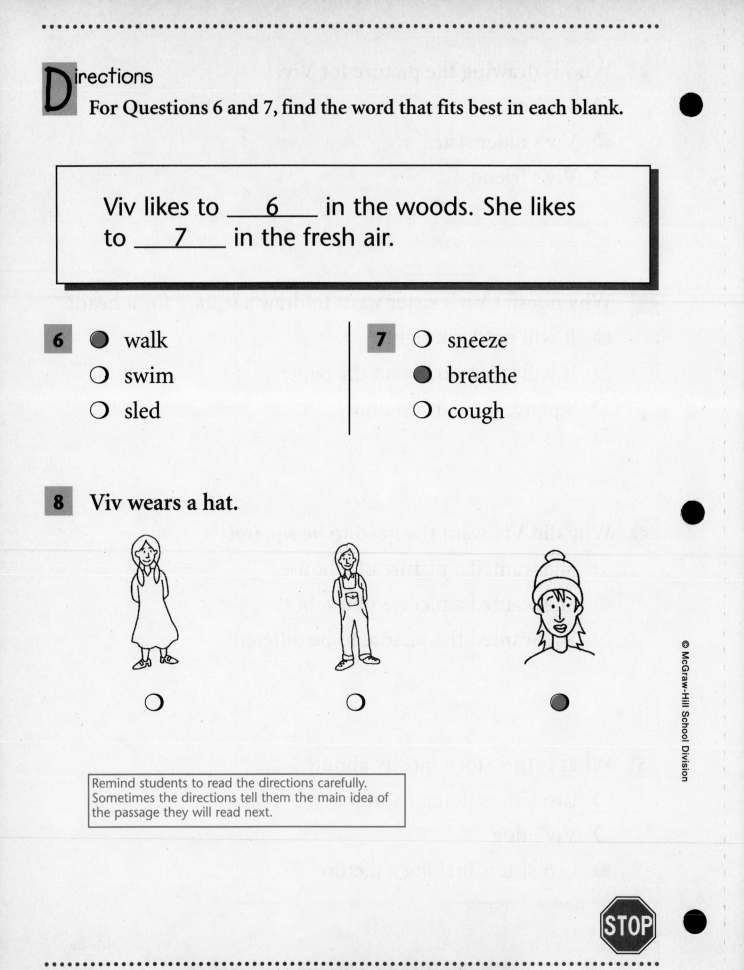

○   ○   ●

Remind students to read the directions carefully. Sometimes the directions tell them the main idea of the passage they will read next.

STOP

Alice Goes to School

Say: *This story is called "Alice Goes to School." It is about a young girl named Alice. She wants to go to school, but she isn't old enough yet. Read the story. Then answer questions 1 through 14.*

Andy and Amy waited for the bus.

They were going to school.

Alice was not old enough for school yet.

"I wish I could go with you," said Alice.

"You are too young," said Andy.

"When you are five you can go," said Amy.

"Try not to miss us, Alice," said Andy. "School isn't easy.
We have to read and write and learn math. And we
have gym, art, and music, too."

"Don't forget about recess!"
said Amy. "That's what I like the most about school."

Alice waved goodbye to Andy and Amy.

"I want to go to school, too," she said.

"We have things to do," said Grandma.

"We need to go to the store."

"I don't want to go," said Alice.

"It will be fun," said Grandma.

"We can pretend it is just like school."

Alice was interested.

She went with Grandma to the store.

At the store, Grandma said, "Let's get
ten apples to make a pie."

"I can count to ten!" said Alice.

She filled up a bag with apples.

"We need fifteen small potatoes for the stew."

"I can count to fifteen!" said Alice.

She put fifteen small potatoes into a bag.

"We'll need a lime and a lemon, too," said Grandma.

"Limes are green and lemons are yellow."

"I know my colors!" said Alice. Alice put a lemon and a
lime into the cart.

On their way out of the store, Alice raised her hand.

"Yes, Alice?" Grandma asked with a grin.

"Is it time for recess?" Alice asked with a giggle.

Say: *Find the answer choices for question 1. Which picture shows what Andy and Amy were doing? Fill in the circle under the picture that shows what they were doing.*

Say: *Find the answer choices for question 2. Why couldn't Alice go to school with Andy and Amy? Fill in the circle next to the best answer to this question.*

TEACHER DIRECTIONS:
Read the answer choices.

Say: *Find the answer choices for question 3. Why did Andy tell Alice that school was not easy?*

TEACHER DIRECTIONS:
Read the answer choices.

Say: *Use what you learned in the story to figure out why Andy said this.*

Exercise 17

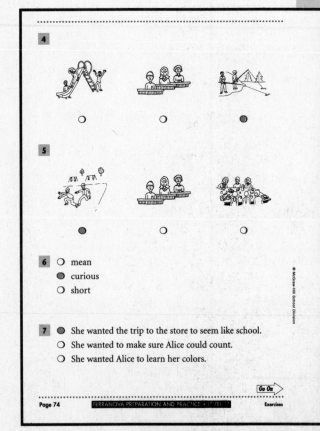

1

2   ○ She had to go to the store.
    ● She was not five yet.
    ○ She had not packed her lunch.

3   ● He wanted to make Alice feel better.
    ○ He liked school.
    ○ He had too much homework.

© McGraw-Hill School Division

Go On →

4

5

6   ○ mean
    ● curious
    ○ short

© McGraw-Hill School Division

7   ● She wanted the trip to the store to seem like school.
    ○ She wanted to make sure Alice could count.
    ○ She wanted Alice to learn her colors.

Go On →

Say: *Find the answer choices for question 4. Which picture shows something Andy and Amy do NOT do when they go to school?*

Say: *Find the answer choices for question 5. Which picture shows what Amy likes the most about school?*

Say: *Find the answer choices for question 6. When Grandma tells Alice that the store will be just like school, Alice was **interested**. What do you think **interested** means?*

TEACHER DIRECTIONS:
Read the answer choices.

Say: *Find the answer choices for question 7. Why do you think Grandma wanted Alice to count ten apples and fifteen potatoes?*

TEACHER DIRECTIONS:
Read the answer choices.

© McGraw-Hill School Division

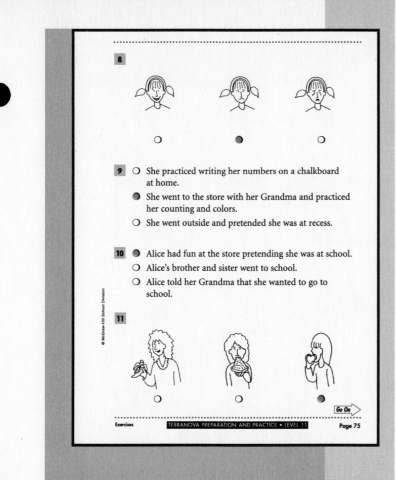

8

9
- ○ She practiced writing her numbers on a chalkboard at home.
- ● She went to the store with her Grandma and practiced her counting and colors.
- ○ She went outside and pretended she was at recess.

10
- ● Alice had fun at the store pretending she was at school.
- ○ Alice's brother and sister went to school.
- ○ Alice told her Grandma that she wanted to go to school.

11

Go On ➡

© McGraw-Hill School Division

Say: *Find the answer choices for question 8. At the end of the story, Alice giggles. Which picture shows how Alice felt at the beginning of the story?*

Say: *Find the answer choices for question 9. How does Alice get to go to school?*

TEACHER DIRECTIONS:
Read the answer choices.

Say: *Find the answer choices for question 10. Which sentence best describes the story?*

TEACHER DIRECTIONS:
Read the answer choices.

Say: *For questions 11 and 12, I will read you a sentence. Then you choose the picture that best shows what the sentence says.*

Say: *Find the answer choices for question 11. Listen carefully as I say the sentence.* **Alice eats an apple.**

Say: *Find the answer choices for question 12. Listen carefully as I say the sentence.* **Andy rides a bicycle.**

Say: *For questions 13 and 14, find the words that best fit in the blanks.*

TEACHER DIRECTIONS:
Read the first sentence and the answer choices for question 13.

TEACHER DIRECTIONS:
Read the second sentence and the answer choices for question 14.

12

At the library, Amy took out a ___13___ for Andy. She knew he liked to ___14___.

13
○ crayon
● book
○ toy

14
● read
○ write
○ play

© McGraw-Hill School Division

STOP

Say: *I am about to read you a poem. It is called "Breakfast Table." It's about a family eating at the breakfast table. Listen carefully as I read it to you. Then answer questions 1 through 13.*

"Breakfast Table"

by Jonathan Yarkony

In the morning, I drink apple juice,
My mom sips a bit of tea,
My brother has some lemonade.
And Daddy, he drinks coffee.

I like a bowl of frosty flakes,
My brother, he likes shredded wheat.

My mom might make an egg or two,
And Daddy has some toast to eat.

We always sit together
And talk about the day ahead,
Share a joke to help each other
Shake the sleep out of our heads.

Say: *Questions 1 through 4 ask you to remember details from the poem. Fill in the circle under the pictures that best answer the questions.*

Say: *Find the answer choices for question 1. Which picture shows what the mom would drink for breakfast?*

Say: *Find the answer choices for question 2. Which shows something the dad does NOT have for breakfast?*

Exercise 18

1

○ ● ○

2

○ ● ○

© McGraw-Hill School Division

Go On

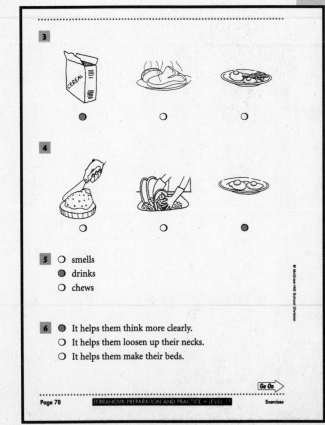

5 ○ smells
   ● drinks
   ○ chews

6 ● It helps them think more clearly.
   ○ It helps them loosen up their necks.
   ○ It helps them make their beds.

© McGraw-Hill School Division

Go On

Say: *Find the answer choices for question 3. Which of the following is the child most likely to eat for breakfast?*

Say: *Find the answer choices for question 4. What does the child's mom make herself for breakfast?*

Say: *The next two questions ask you to figure out what a word or phrase means.*

Say: *Find the answer choices for question 5. The poem says "My mom sips a bit of tea." Which word means about the same as sips?*

TEACHER DIRECTIONS:
Read the answer choices.

Say: *Find the answer choices for question 6. The poem says that talking around the table helps the family "shake the sleep out of our heads." What do you think "shake the sleep out of our heads" means?*

TEACHER DIRECTIONS:
Read the answer choices.

© McGraw-Hill School Division

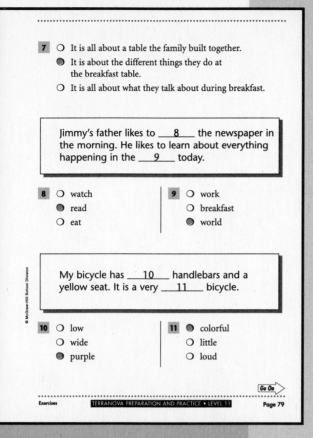

7 ○ It is all about a table the family built together.
   ● It is about the different things they do at the breakfast table.
   ○ It is all about what they talk about during breakfast.

Jimmy's father likes to __8__ the newspaper in the morning. He likes to learn about everything happening in the __9__ today.

8 ○ watch
   ● read
   ○ eat

9 ○ work
   ○ breakfast
   ● world

My bicycle has __10__ handlebars and a yellow seat. It is a very __11__ bicycle.

10 ○ low
   ○ wide
   ● purple

11 ● colorful
   ○ little
   ○ loud

© McGraw-Hill School Division

Go On ⇨

Say: *Find the answer choices for question 7. Why do you think "Breakfast Table" is a good name for this poem?*

TEACHER DIRECTIONS:
Read the answer choices.

Say: *For questions 8 and 9, find the words that best fit in the blanks.*

TEACHER DIRECTIONS:
Read the first sentence and the answer choices for question 8.

TEACHER DIRECTIONS:
Read the second sentence and the answer choices for question 9.

Say: *For questions 10 and 11, find the words that best fit in the blanks. Sometimes you might have to read the second sentence in order to find the word that fits in the blank of the first sentence.*

TEACHER DIRECTIONS:
Read the first sentence and the answer choices for question 10.

TEACHER DIRECTIONS:
Read the second sentence and the answer choices for question 11.

Say: *For the last two questions, I will read you a sentence. Then you choose the picture that best shows what the sentence says.*

Say: *Find the answer choices for question 12. Listen carefully as I say the sentence.* **See the refrigerator.**

Say: *Find the answer choices for question 13. Listen carefully as I say the sentence.* **Sheila cooks eggs.**

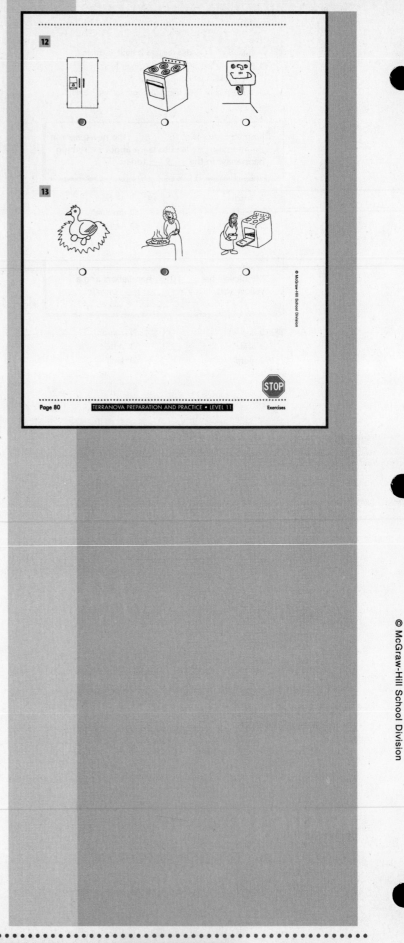

"My Crazy Cockatoo"

by Jonathan Yarkony

My crazy cockatoo
is a handsome fellow.
He likes to perch
and sit in a hollow,
flap his wings like
a bird caught on fire,
hopping and chirping
like he'll never ever tire.

This madcap cockatoo
has quite a crown.
He can raise it at will,
and fold it back down.
When he spreads it out
he might be warning you,
but he might also be asking
for something to chew.

Say: *The poem I am about to read to you is called "My Crazy Cockatoo." A cockatoo is a kind of bird. Some people have cockatoos as pets. Listen carefully as I read the poem to you. Then answer the questions.*

Say: *Find the answer choices for question 1. What does a cockatoo look like? Fill in the circle under the picture that shows what a cockatoo looks like.*

Say: *Find the answer choices for question 2. What does the crazy cockatoo like to do?*

Say: *Find the answer choices for question 3. What do you think <u>chirping</u> means in the lines, "hopping and <u>chirping</u> like he'll never tire"?*

TEACHER DIRECTIONS:
Read the answer choices.

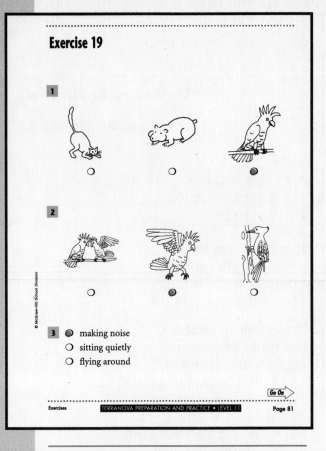

3
- ● making noise
- ○ sitting quietly
- ○ flying around

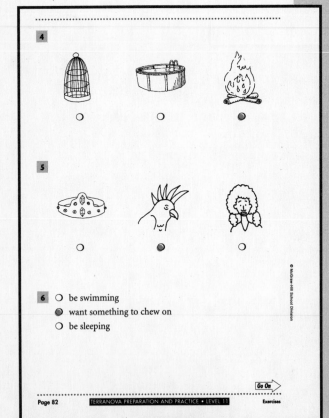

6
- ○ be swimming
- ● want something to chew on
- ○ be sleeping

Say: *Find the answer choices for question 4. Fill in the circle under the picture that best completes the following sentence. The cockatoo is described as acting like a bird caught on—*

Say: *Find the answer choices for question 5. The poem says that the cockatoo has a <u>crown</u> that he can raise and then fold back down. What do you think his <u>crown</u> looks like?*

Say: *Find the answer choices for question 6. Using what you learned in the story, fill in the circle next to the answer that best completes the following sentence. If the cockatoo has his crown up, it means that he might—*

TEACHER INSTRUCTIONS:
Read the answer choices.

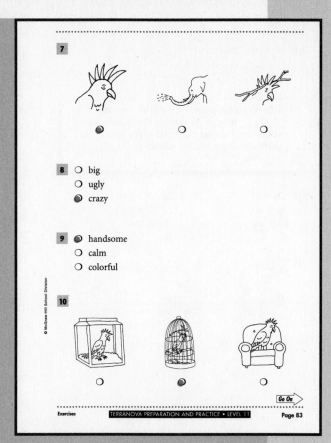

7

8 ○ big
○ ugly
● crazy

9 ● handsome
○ calm
○ colorful

10

Go On →

© McGraw-Hill School Division

Say: *Find the answer choices for question 7. What can the cockatoo do with his crown?*

Say: *Find the answer choices for question 8. What does* <u>madcap</u> *mean in the line, "This* <u>madcap</u> *cockatoo has quite a crown"?*

TEACHER DIRECTIONS:
Read the answer choices.

Say: *Find the answer choices for question 9. Using what you learned in the story, fill in the circle next to the answer that best completes the following sentence. The owner of the cockatoo thinks his bird is—*

TEACHER DIRECTIONS:
Read the answer choices.

Say: *Find the answer choices for question 10. Where does this cockatoo probably live?*

Say: *Find the answer choices for question 11. What would be another good name for this poem?*

TEACHER DIRECTIONS:
Read the answer choices.

Say: *For questions 12 and 13, find the words that best fit in the blanks.*

TEACHER DIRECTIONS:
Read the first sentence and the answer choices for question 12.

TEACHER DIRECTIONS:
Read the second sentence and the answer choices for question 13.

Say: *For question 14, I will read you a sentence. Then you choose the picture that best shows what the sentence says.*

Say: *Find the answer choices for question 14. Listen carefully as I say the sentence.* **See Emmanuel walk the dog.**

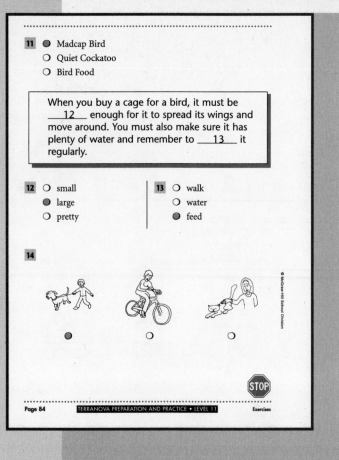

11 ● Madcap Bird
   ○ Quiet Cockatoo
   ○ Bird Food

When you buy a cage for a bird, it must be ___12___ enough for it to spread its wings and move around. You must also make sure it has plenty of water and remember to ___13___ it regularly.

12 ○ small
   ● large
   ○ pretty

13 ○ walk
   ○ water
   ● feed

14

Page 84   TERRANOVA PREPARATION AND PRACTICE • LEVEL 11   Exercises

The Big Cheese

Mouse teased Little Ant. "I am much bigger than you!" he said. They were waiting in line for a piece of the cheese that Rat found.

"If that is so, you may go ahead of me," said Little Ant as he moved aside to let Mouse pass.

Mouse then teased Little Bug who was next in line. "I am much hungrier than you!" he said.

"If that is so, you may go ahead of me," said Little Bug.

Mouse then teased Fly, who was next in line. "I need more food than you!" he said.

"If that is so, you may go ahead of me," said Fly. Pretty soon, Mouse was the first one in line. He was sure that now he would get the biggest piece of cheese.

"This is how I will divide my cheese," said Rat. "The first one in line will get the smallest piece, and the last one in line will get the biggest."

Say: *The story I am about to read you is about an ant, mouse, fly, and bug. They were in line waiting for the rat to give them a piece of cheese. Listen carefully as I read the story to you. Then answer questions 1 through 12.*

© McGraw-Hill School Division

Say: *Find the answer choices for question 1. How did Mouse move ahead of all the others in line?*

TEACHER DIRECTIONS:
Read the answer choices.

Say: *Find the answer choices for question 2. In the beginning of the story, Mouse was the last in line. Why did he want to be the first one in line?*

TEACHER DIRECTIONS:
Read the answer choices.

Say: *Find the answer choices for question 3. Who was the second one that Mouse moved ahead of?*

TEACHER DIRECTIONS:
Read the answer choices.

Say: *Find the answer choices for question 4. In the story, Rat says, "Here is how I will divide my cheese." A word that means almost the same thing as divide is—*

TEACHER DIRECTIONS:
Read the answer choices.

Exercise 20

1
- He teased them.
- ○ He asked them.
- ○ He tricked them.

2
- ○ He thought he was the hungriest.
- ○ He was Rat's best friend.
- He thought he would get the biggest piece of cheese.

3
- ○ Rat
- Little Bug
- ○ Little Ant

4
- separate
- ○ whole
- ○ cook

Go On ▷

© McGraw-Hill School Division

Say: *Find the answer choices for Question 5. Mouse had a plan that he would be rewarded for being the first in line. If his plan had worked, what would have been Mouse's reward? Fill in the circle that shows what reward Mouse would have gotten.*

Say: *Find the answer choices for question 6. What happened when Mouse teased Little Ant?*

TEACHER DIRECTIONS:
Read the answer choices.

Say: *Question 7 asks you to think about the end of the story. Which sentence best completes the story?*

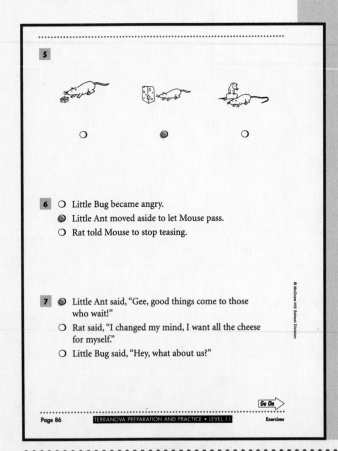

5
○   ●   ○

6
- ○ Little Bug became angry.
- Little Ant moved aside to let Mouse pass.
- ○ Rat told Mouse to stop teasing.

7
- Little Ant said, "Gee, good things come to those who wait!"
- ○ Rat said, "I changed my mind, I want all the cheese for myself."
- ○ Little Bug said, "Hey, what about us?"

© McGraw-Hill School Division

Go On ▷

© McGraw-Hill School Division

8

○   ○   ●

Little Ant ___9___ in line. He wanted a
___10___ of cheese.

9
- ○ hurried
- ● waited
- ○ sat

10
- ○ crumb
- ○ bag
- ● piece

Go On

© McGraw-Hill School Division

Say: *Question 8 asks you to figure out what the whole story is about, not just part of the story. Which picture shows what happened in the story?*

Say: *For questions 9 and 10, find the word that fits best in each blank.*

TEACHER DIRECTIONS:
Read the first sentence and the answer choices for question 9.

TEACHER DIRECTIONS:
Read the second sentence and the answer choices for question 10.

Say: *For questions 11 and 12, I will read you a sentence. Then you choose the picture that best shows what the sentence says.*

Say: *Find the answer choices for question 11. Listen carefully as I say the sentence.* **See the man bake a cake.**

Say: *Find the answer choices for question 12. Listen carefully as I say the sentence.* **The girl has socks that don't match.**

Exercise 21

Go On

Say: Find question number 1. Fill in the circle next to the answer choice that correctly changes the first sentence into a question.

1 My mother is at work.
- ● Is my mother at work?
- ○ My mother at work is?
- ○ At my mother work is?

Say: Find question number 2. Fill in the circle next to the punctuation mark that goes best in the blank.

2 Dear Doris and Cynthia ___
- ● ,
- ○ .
- ○ ?

Say: Find question number 3. Fill in the circle under the part of the sentence that has an error in punctuation or capitalization.

3 The team   won   the game,
     ○   ○   ●

Say: Find question number 4. Fill in the circle next to the word that completes the sentence correctly.

4 Paul helped _____ to the snacks.

- ○ them
- ○ he
- ● himself

Say: Find question number 5. Fill in the circle next to the word that can take the place of the underlined words.

5 <u>You and I</u> swim in the lake.

- ○ They
- ○ You
- ● We

Say: In questions 6 and 7, the sentences start to tell a story, but the story is not finished. First, find question number 6. Fill in the circle next to the sentence that best finishes the story.

6 Maria wants to draw.
Maria gets paper.

_____.

- ○ Maria likes to sing.
- ○ Maria reads a book.
- ● Maria picks a crayon.

Go On

Say: Now find question number 7, and find the circle next to the sentence that best finishes the story.

7 Scott gets ready for bed.
He brushes his teeth.

_____.

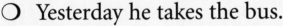

○ Then he eats dinner.

● He puts on his pajamas.

○ Scott helps wash the dishes.

Say: For questions 8 and 9, fill in the circle next to the sentence that is complete and correct. First, find question number 8. Fill in the circle next to the sentence that is complete and correct.

8 ○ The children takes the bus to school.

○ Yesterday he takes the bus.

● They take the bus every day.

Say: Now find question number 9, and fill in the circle next to the sentence that is complete and correct.

9 ○ If Fred buys a new shirt.

● Wendy buys a new dress for the party.

○ They buys cake and soda for the party.

Go On

Say: Find question number 10. Then fill in the circle that is below the word with the same vowel sound as <u>map</u>.

10   dog   hat   hits
          ○   ●   ○

Say: Find question number 11. Then fill in the circle below the word <u>lick</u>.

11   lick   lit   lap
          ●   ○   ○

Say: Find question number 12. Then fill in the circle that is below the word with the same vowel sound as <u>rip</u>.

12   mop   cap   sit
          ○   ○   ●

Exercise 22

Say: Find question number 1. Fill in the circle next to the answer choice that correctly turns the first sentence into a question.

1 He was Tara's dog.

○ Tara's he was dog?

○ He Tara's dog is?

● Is he Tara's dog?

Say: Find question number 2. Fill in the circle under the part of the sentence that has an error in punctuation or capitalization.

2 Mark and fred   played   soccer.
        ●   ○   ○

Say: Find question number 3. Fill in the circle next to the punctuation mark that best fits in the blank.

3 Choose a partner ____

● .

○ ?

○ ,

Say: Find question number 4. Fill in the circle next to the word that correctly completes the sentence.

4 Please let _____ into the house.

- ● yourself
- ○ they
- ○ I

Say: Find question number 5. Fill in the circle next to the word that can take the place of the underlined word.

5 Tom asked <u>Steve</u> to play tag.

- ○ he
- ● him
- ○ her

Say: In questions 6 and 7, the sentences start to tell a story, but the story is not finished. First find question number 6. Fill in the circle next to the sentence that best finishes the story.

6 Terrence studied for his spelling test. He wrote down all the words.

_____.

- ● His mother helped him practice the words.
- ○ He watched his favorite television show.
- ○ Then he practiced playing his drums.

Say: Now find question number 7, and fill in the circle next to the sentence that best finishes the story.

7 Betty cleans her room.
First she makes her bed.

_____.

○ Then she makes a cake.

● Then she puts away her toys.

○ Then she calls her best friend.

Say: For questions 8 and 9, fill in the circle next to the sentence that is complete and correct. First find question number 8. Fill in the circle next to the sentence that is complete and correct.

8 ● Marta played in the park.

○ After the boys play.

○ The girls plays with the puppy.

Say: Now find question number 9, and fill in the circle next to the sentence that is complete and correct.

9 ○ He visit his Uncle Paul last week.

○ Before they visit the zoo.

● Gus visits his grandmother.

Say: Find question number 10. Then fill in the circle below the word with the same beginning sound as <u>shoe</u>.

10   <u>sh</u>op   <u>s</u>ip   <u>s</u>ad
         ●   ○   ○

Say: Find question number 11. Then fill in the circle below the word with the same beginning sound as <u>them</u>.

11   <u>t</u>in   <u>th</u>is   <u>t</u>op
         ○   ●   ○

Say: Find question number 12. Then fill in the circle below the word <u>bus</u>.

12   big   bat   bus
         ○   ○   ●

© McGraw-Hill School Division

Exercise 23

Say: Find question number 1. Fill in the circle next to the answer choice that correctly turns the first sentence into a question.

1 We were here first.
- ○ We here first were?
- ● Were we here first?
- ○ Here we were first?

Say: Find question number 2. Fill in the circle under the section of the sentence that contains an error in punctuation or capitalization.

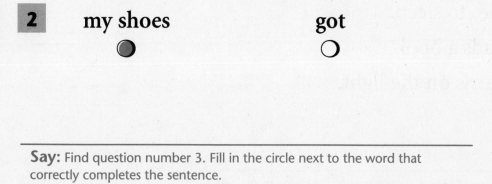

2 my shoes   got   muddy.
    ●   ○   ○

Say: Find question number 3. Fill in the circle next to the word that correctly completes the sentence.

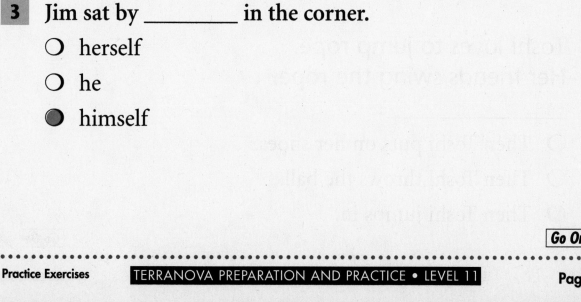

3 Jim sat by _____ in the corner.
- ○ herself
- ○ he
- ● himself

© McGraw-Hill School Division

Say: Find question number 4. Fill in the circle next to the word that can take the place of the underlined words.

4 <u>The clouds</u> moved across the sky.

● They

○ It

○ Them

Say: In questions 5 and 6, the sentences start to tell a story, but the story is not finished. First find question number 5. Fill in the circle next to the sentence that best finishes the story.

5 It is late.
Jana is tired.

_____.

● She goes to sleep.

○ She reads a book.

○ Jana turns on the light.

Say: Now find question number 6 and fill in the circle next to the sentence that best finishes the story.

6 Toshi loves to jump rope.
Her friends swing the rope.

_____.

○ Then Toshi puts on her shoes.

○ Then Toshi throws the ball.

● Then Toshi jumps in.

Go On

Say: For questions 7 and 8, fill in the circle next to the sentence that is complete and correct. First find question number 7. Fill in the circle next to the sentence that is complete and correct.

7
- ● The farmer works on the tractor.
- ○ Sally work at the store yesterday.
- ○ Once Sally works.

Say: Now find question number 8, and fill in the circle next to the sentence that is complete and correct.

8
- ○ He lick the grape lollipop.
- ○ When Pat licks the stamp.
- ● The boy licks the ice cream cone.

Say: Find question number 9. Then fill in the circle that is below the word with the same vowel sound as <u>hot</u>.

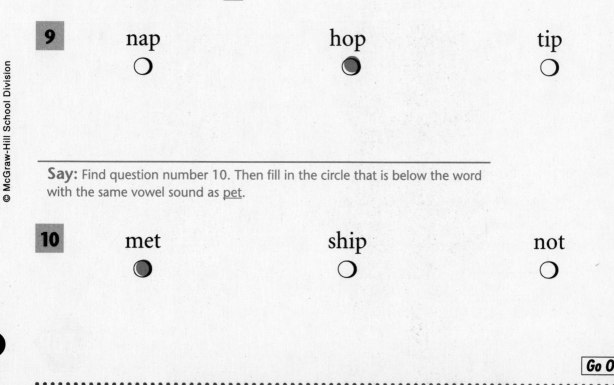

9

nap	hop	tip
○	●	○

Say: Find question number 10. Then fill in the circle that is below the word with the same vowel sound as <u>pet</u>.

10

met	ship	not
●	○	○

Say: Find question number 11. Then fill in the circle below the word with the same beginning sound as <u>flower</u>.

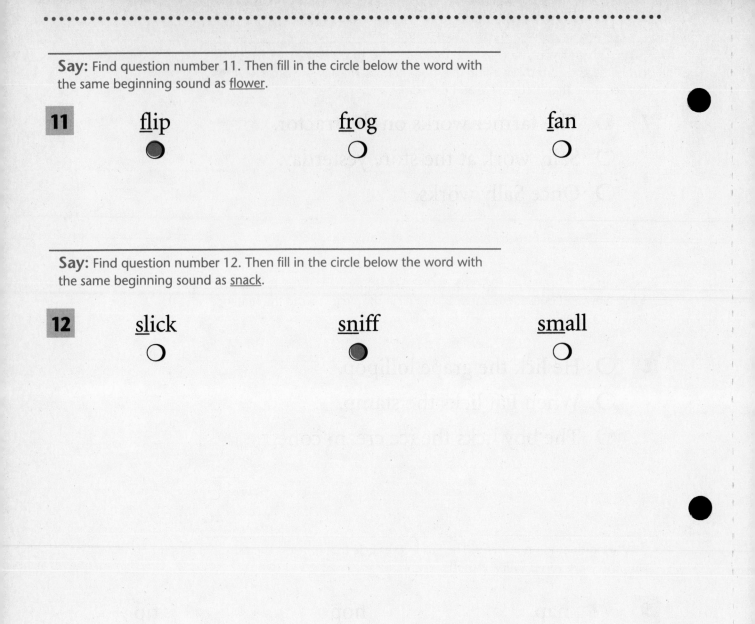

11   <u>fl</u>ip   <u>fr</u>og   <u>f</u>an

            ●   ○   ○

Say: Find question number 12. Then fill in the circle below the word with the same beginning sound as <u>snack</u>.

12   <u>sl</u>ick   <u>sn</u>iff   <u>sm</u>all

            ○   ●   ○

Exercise 24

Say: Find question number 1. Fill in the circle next to the answer choice that correctly turns the first sentence into a question.

1 Pedro and Gus are best friends.

- ● Are Pedro and Gus best friends?
- ○ Pedro and Gus best friends are?
- ○ Best Pedro and Gus are friends?

Say: Find question number 2. Fill in the circle under the part of the sentence that has an error in punctuation or capitalization.

2

Carl   went with Us   to the movies.
○   ●   ○

Say: Find question number 3. Fill in the circle next to the word that correctly completes the sentence.

3 Give _____ a rest if you get tired.

- ○ you
- ● yourself
- ○ herself

Say: Find question number 4. Fill in the circle next to the word that can take the place of the underlined word.

4 One piece of cake is for <u>Kathy</u>.

- ● her
- ○ she
- ○ you

Say: In questions 5 and 6, the sentences start to tell a story, but the story is not finished. First find question number 5. Fill in the circle next to the sentence that best finishes the story.

5 Jose's dog ran away.
Jose looked for him.

_____.

- ○ Jose likes playing with his friends.
- ● The dog came home soon.
- ○ Dogs do not get along with cats.

Say: Now find question number 6, and fill in the circle next to the sentence that best finishes the story.

6 The class visits the zoo.
They see the monkeys.

_____.

- ● They look at the lions.
- ○ The class plays on the swings.
- ○ They want to see the movie.

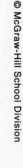

TERRANOVA PREPARATION AND PRACTICE • LEVEL 11   **Practice Exercises**

Say: For questions 7 and 8, fill in the circle next to the sentence that is complete and correct. First find question number 7. Fill in the circle next to the sentence that is complete and correct.

7 ● I meet my mother at school.
   ○ After he meets his mother.
   ○ She meets me last week.

Say: Now find question number 8 and fill in the circle next to the sentence that is complete and correct.

8 ○ When the player hits the ball out of the park.
   ○ They hits the ball for practice.
   ● Harold hits the ball out of the park.

Say: Find question number 9. Then fill in the circle below the word <u>hand</u>.

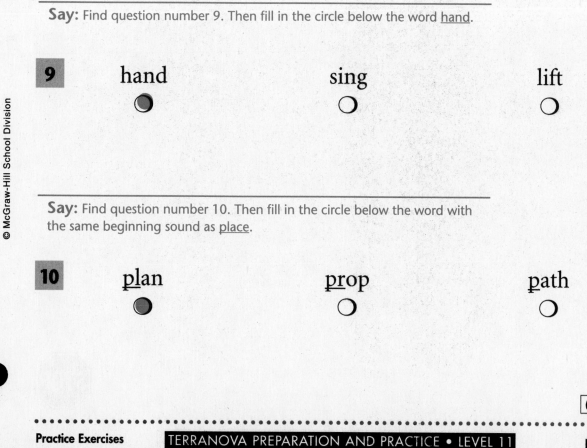

9   hand   sing   lift
      ●   ○   ○

Say: Find question number 10. Then fill in the circle below the word with the same beginning sound as <u>place</u>.

10   plan   prop   path
      ●   ○   ○

••

Say: Find question number 11. Then fill in the circle below the word with the same beginning sound as <u>check</u>.

11   <u>cr</u>ab   <u>c</u>up   <u>chip</u>
       ○   ○   ●

Say: Find question number 12. Then fill in the circle below the word <u>tape</u>.

12   tall   tag   tape
       ○   ○   ●

STOP

Exercise 25

Say: Find question number 1. Fill in the circle next to the answer choice that correctly turns the first sentence into a question.

1 **Ben is the fastest runner.**
- ○ Ben the fastest runner is?
- ○ The fastest Ben is runner?
- ● Is Ben the fastest runner?

Say: Find question number 2. Fill in the circle under the part of the sentence that has an error in punctuation or capitalization.

2   **dear**   **Mrs.**   **Jones,**
           ●   ○   ○

Say: Find question number 3. Fill in the circle next to the punctuation mark that correctly fills in the blank.

3 **Thank you for the gift ___**
- ○ ,
- ● .
- ○ ?

Say: Find question number 4. Fill in the circle next to the word that correctly completes the sentence.

4 Ed wrote a letter to _____.

○ she

○ itself

● her

Say: Find question number 5. Fill in the circle next to the word that can take the place of the underlined words.

5 Daddy bought a new dollhouse for <u>Beth and me</u>.

○ we

○ her

● us

Say: In questions 6 and 7, the sentences start to tell a story, but the story is not finished. First find question number 6. Fill in the circle next to the sentence that best finishes the story.

6 George makes a peanut butter and jelly sandwich. George spreads the peanut butter.

_____.

○ Then he draws a picture.

○ George likes to eat popcorn.

● Then he puts on the jelly.

Go On

Say: Now find question number 7 and fill in the circle next to the sentence that best finishes the story.

7 The boy made a paper airplane.
He folded the paper a few times.

_____.

- ○ Then he threw the ball to his friend.
- ● Then he threw it in the air.
- ○ The boy likes airplanes.

Say: For questions 8 and 9, fill in the circle next to the sentence that is complete and correct. First find question number 8. Fill in the circle next to the sentence that is complete and correct.

8
- ● Lola notices the boy in the corner.
- ○ She notice the spot on her shirt after dinner.
- ○ If she notices the mistake.

Say: Now find question number 9 and fill in the circle next to the sentence that is complete and correct.

9
- ○ When the clown gives her a gift.
- ○ The clown give her some popcorn.
- ● The clown gives her a balloon.

Go On

Say: Find question number 10. Then fill in the circle that is below the word with the same vowel sound as <u>wave</u>.

10   tank   snap   gave
            ○   ○   ●

Say: Find question number 11. Then fill in the circle that is below the word with the same vowel sound as <u>hide</u>.

11   hiss   wide   bigger
            ○   ●   ○

Say: Find question number 12. Then fill in the circle that is below the word with the same vowel sound as <u>note</u>.

12   rope   flop   shop
            ●   ○   ○

Exercise 26

Go On →

Say: Find question number 1. Fill in the circle next to the answer choice that correctly turns the first sentence into a question.

1 I am Rita's cousin.
- ○ Rita's I am cousin?
- ● Am I Rita's cousin?
- ○ I Rita's cousin am?

Say: Find question number 2. Fill in the circle under the part of the sentence that has an error in punctuation or capitalization.

2 Love,   miss   Parker
       ○   ●   ○

Say: Find question number 3. Fill in the circle next to the punctuation mark that correctly fills in the blank.

3 Please write back ____
- ○ ?
- ○ ,
- ● .

Say: Find question number 4. Fill in the circle next to the word that correctly completes the sentence.

4 My sister and _____ jumped rope.

   ○ me

   ○ herself

   ● I

Say: Find question number 5. Fill in the circle next to the word that can take the place of the underlined words.

5 <u>My uncle</u> works in the city.

   ○ I

   ○ Him

   ● He

Say: In questions 6, 7, and 8, the sentences start to tell a story, but the story is not finished. First find question number 6. Fill in the circle next to the sentence that best finishes the story.

6 My mother is an artist.
She paints many things.

_____.

   ● I like her paintings of animals.

   ○ She takes care of my pet hamster.

   ○ She likes to play tennis.

Say: Now find question number 7. Fill in the circle next to the sentence that best finishes the story.

7 Pam goes to the library
Pam finds a good book.

_____.

○ She wants to be a doctor .

● She checks out the book.

○ Then she finds a good toy.

Say: Now find question number 8. Fill in the circle next to the sentence that best finishes the story.

8 Ina gets ready for school.
She packs her backpack.

_____.

● Then she goes to the bus stop.

○ She makes sure she has her ice skates.

○ Her best subject is math.

Say: For questions 9 and 10, fill in the circle next to the sentence that is complete and correct. First find question number 9. Fill in the circle next to the sentence that is complete and correct.

9 ● Patty sees her friend every day.

○ Patty and Lisa sees the toy on the floor.

○ Lisa see the girl at school.

© McGraw-Hill School Division

Say: Now find question number 10, and fill in the circle next to the sentence that is complete and correct.

10
- ○ When we go to the store.
- ○ You and I goes to the movies.
- ● We go together.

Say: Find question number 11. Then fill in the circle that is below the word with the same vowel sound as <u>due</u>.

11   dump   clue   duck
          ○   ●   ○

Say: Find question number 12. Then fill in the circle that is below the word with the same vowel sound as <u>late</u>.

12   mat   call   wait
          ○   ○   ●

Exercise 27

Say: Find question number 1. Fill in the circle next to the answer choice that correctly turns the first sentence into a question.

1 You are a good singer.

- ● Are you a good singer?
- ○ A good singer you are.
- ○ A good you are singer?

Say: Find question number 2. Fill in the circle under the section of the sentence that contains an error in punctuation or capitalization.

2   How   are   You?
       ○   ○   ●

Say: Find question number 3. Fill in the circle next to the punctuation mark that correctly fills in the blank.

3 Hold on to the rope _____

- ○ ?
- ● .
- ○ ,

Say: Find question number 4. Fill in the circle next to the word that correctly completes the sentence.

4 Nancy left _____ at the mall.

● him

○ he

○ himself

Say: Find question number 5. Fill in the circle next to the word that can take the place of the underlined words.

5 Terry fed <u>the cat and the dog</u>.

● them

○ it

○ they

Say: In questions 6 and 7, the sentences start to tell a story, but the story is not finished. First find question number 6. Fill in the circle next to the sentence that best completes the story.

6 Sheila and Didi build a sandcastle. They make the walls of the castle. _____.

● Then they dig a moat around it.

○ Then they paint flowers.

○ They read the story about the princess.

Say: Now find question number 7 and fill in the circle next to the sentence that best completes the story.

7 Ronnie draws a picture of a cat.
He colors in the cat's face.

_____.

- ◯ He has a friend who likes animals.
- ◯ Cats make good pets.
- ⬤ Then he draws in the whiskers.

Say: For questions 8 and 9, fill in the circle next to the sentence that is complete and correct. First find question number 8. Fill in the circle next to the sentence that is complete and correct.

8
- ◯ He comes last week.
- ⬤ Henry and Juan come to school.
- ◯ Before they come into the classroom.

Say: Now find question number 9 and fill in the circle next to the sentence that is complete and correct.

9
- ◯ If David is a good player.
- ◯ They is going to play on Friday.
- ⬤ David is the best player.

© McGraw-Hill School Division

Go On ⟹

Say: Find question number 10. Then fill in the circle below the word <u>week</u>.

10   went   week   wet
   ○   ●   ○

Say: Find question number 11. Then fill in the circle below the word <u>peach</u>.

11   pump   peach   pill
   ○   ●   ○

Say: Find question number 12. Then fill in the circle below the word <u>sight</u>.

12   sight   slipping   show
   ●   ○   ○

STOP

Exercise 28

Go On

Say: Find question number 1. Fill in the circle next to the answer choice that correctly turns the first sentence into a question.

1 Dina was Miss Smith's favorite student.
- ○ Miss Smith's favorite Dina was student?
- ○ Miss Smith's favorite student Dina was?
- ● Was Dina Miss Smith's favorite student?

Say: Find question number 2. Fill in the circle under the section of the sentence that contains an error in punctuation or capitalization.

2 the store   was   closed.
    ●   ○   ○

Say: Find question number 3. Fill in the circle next to the punctuation mark that correctly fills in the blank.

3 How old are you _____
- ○ .
- ● ?
- ○ ,

Say: Find question number 4. Fill in the circle next to the word that correctly completes the sentence.

4 _____ were late to the meeting.

○ Them

● They

○ Us

Say: Find question number 5. Fill in the circle next to the word that can take the place of the underlined word.

5 <u>Singing</u> is my favorite thing to do.

○ He

● It

○ You

Say: In questions 6 and 7, the sentences start to tell a story, but the story is not finished. First find question number 6. Fill in the circle next to the sentence that best completes the story.

6 Tito has many toys.
He has building blocks and toy cars.
_____.

○ Tito likes to play football and baseball.

○ He has a pet goldfish.

● His favorite toy is a toy truck.

© McGraw-Hill School Division

Say: Now find question number 7 and fill in the circle next to the sentence that best completes the story.

7 It is raining today.
I put on my raincoat.

_____.

○ I put on my sunglasses.

● Then I found my umbrella.

○ It is a good day for a picnic.

Say: For question 8, fill in the circle next to the sentence that is complete and correct. First find question number 8. Fill in the circle next to the sentence that is complete and correct.

8 ● I want to go to her house.

○ Before I want help.

○ He and I want help last week.

Say: Now find question number 9. Fill in the circle next to the sentence that is below the word with the same vowel sound as rope.

9 rock   hoped   pop
      ○   ●   ○

Go On ▸

Say: Find question number 10. Then fill in the circle that is below the word with the same vowel sound as <u>tool</u>.

10   toad   food   log
         ○   ●   ○

Say: Find question number 11. Then fill in the circle that is below the word with the same vowel sound as <u>cart</u>.

11   part   cat   make
         ●   ○   ○

Say: Find question number 12. Then fill in the circle that is below the word with the same vowel sound as <u>work</u>.

12   bird   spin   bike
         ●   ○   ○

Exercise 29

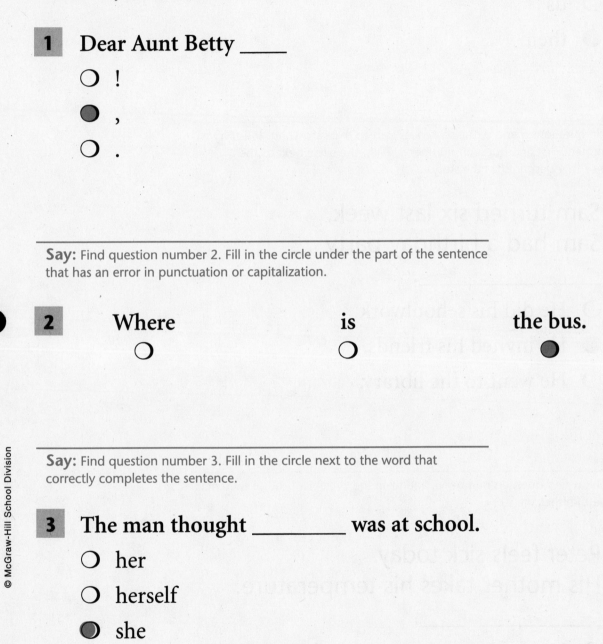

Say: Find question number 1. Fill in the circle next to the punctuation mark that correctly fills in the blank.

1 **Dear Aunt Betty** ____

○ !

● ,

○ .

Say: Find question number 2. Fill in the circle under the part of the sentence that has an error in punctuation or capitalization.

2 **Where** **is** **the bus.**

○ ○ ●

Say: Find question number 3. Fill in the circle next to the word that correctly completes the sentence.

3 **The man thought** _____ **was at school.**

○ her

○ herself

● she

Go On →

Say: Find question number 4. Fill in the circle next to the word that can take the place of the underlined words.

4 **Bill asked <u>the boys</u> to help clean up.**

  ○ him

  ○ us

  ● them

Say: In questions 5 and 6, the sentences start to tell a story, but the story is not finished. First find question number 5. Fill in the circle next to the sentence that best finishes the story.

5 Sam turned six last week.
Sam had a birthday party.

_____.

  ○ He did his schoolwork.

  ● He invited his friends.

  ○ He went to the library.

Say: Now find question number 6, and fill in the circle next to the sentence that best finishes the story.

6 Peter feels sick today.
His mother takes his temperature.

_____.

  ● He needs to take some medicine.

  ○ Peter loves to play football.

  ○ He takes piano lessons after school.

© McGraw-Hill School Division

Say: For questions 7, 8, and 9, fill in the circle next to the sentence that is complete and correct. First find question number 7. Fill in the circle next to the sentence that is complete and correct.

7 ● Tyrone and Dan sit together.

○ They sit on the bus yesterday.

○ After Tyrone sits in the chair.

Say: Now find question number 8 and fill in the circle next to the sentence that is complete and correct.

8 ○ He shows me last March.

● My brother shows me his toy.

○ I shows him the room.

Say: Now find question number 9 and fill in the circle next to the sentence that is complete and correct.

9 ○ Mario and Rick likes art class.

● Mario likes to draw pictures.

○ When Mario likes a picture.

Go On

Say: Find question number 10. Then fill in the circle that is below the word with the same vowel sound as <u>how</u>.

10
soap ○

house ●

sock ○

Say: Find question number 11. Then fill in the circle that is below the word with the same vowel sound as <u>toy</u>.

11
nose ○

spot ○

boy ●

Say: Find question number 12. Then fill in the circle that is below the word <u>cow</u>.

12
mouth ○

cow ●

coin ○

Exercise 30

Say: Find question number 1. Then fill in the circle next to the punctuation mark that correctly fills in the blank.

1 Your friend _____ Elizabeth

○ ?

○ .

● ,

Say: Find question number 2. Fill in the circle under the part of the sentence that has an error in punctuation or capitalization.

2 Her name   is   maria.
     ○   ○   ●

Say: Find question number 3. Fill in the circle next to the word that correctly completes the sentence.

3 _____ ran as fast as he could.

● He

○ Him

○ She

Say: Find question number 4. Fill in the circle next to the word that can take the place of the underlined words.

4 <u>Renee and I</u> raced to the finish line.
- ○ She
- ○ Us
- ● We

Say: In questions 5 and 6, the sentences start to tell a story, but the story is not finished. First find question number 5. Fill in the circle next to the sentence that best finishes the story.

5 Carla is good at sports.
She is on the soccer team.

_____.

- ○ She also likes to sing.
- ○ Carla goes to the playground
- ● The team practices every day.

Say: Now find question number 6, and fill in the circle next to the sentence that best finishes the story.

6 Melissa and Gina are pen pals.
Melissa writes to Gina.

_____.

- ○ Then Gina calls her friends.
- ○ Melissa and Gina like to write letters.
- ● Then Gina writes back.

Go On →

Say: For questions 7, 8, 9, and 10, fill in the circle next to the sentence that is complete and correct. First, find question number 7. Fill in the circle next to the sentence that is complete and correct.

7 ● Now Sheila gives me a smile.

○ Sheila give a present at the party.

○ Because she gives a present.

Say: Now find question number 8 and fill in the circle next to the sentence that is complete and correct.

8 ○ Before they plant seeds.

○ Ping plant seeds in the spring.

● Ping and Joe plant a garden.

Say: Now find question number 9, and fill in the circle next to the sentence that is complete and correct.

9 ○ Opal decides not to swim last week.

○ If she decides to swim.

● Opal decides to swim in the lake.

Say: Find question number 10. Fill in the circle next to the sentence that is complete and correct.

10
- ○ Lana and Eva calls me last night.
- ● They call me at home.
- ○ If Lana and Eva call me.

Say: Find question number 11. Fill in the circle below the word <u>fly</u>.

11

feet	flip	fly
○	○	●

Say: Find question number 12. Fill in the circle below the word <u>train</u>.

12

treat	the	train
○	○	●

Reading and Language Arts

Sample A

Who is Toby Turtle babysitting?

○   ○   ●

Sample B

Toby Turtle _____.

- ● read a book
- ○ great babysitter
- ○ them a snack

Sample C

The next time Mother Mouse needs to go out, she will probably

- ○ bring the baby mice with her
- ● ask Toby Turtle to babysit again
- ○ find a new babysitter

STOP

© McGraw-Hill School Division

TEACHER DIRECTIONS:
Before your students start the Practice Test, read the following passage and work through the sample questions together.

Say: *Now I will read aloud a story about Toby Turtle baby-sitting.*

Toby Turtle played with the baby mice. He was babysitting while Mother Mouse was out collecting food. First, they played a game. Then, Toby read them a book. Finally, Toby gave them a snack. When Mother Mouse came home, the baby mice didn't want Toby to leave. He was a great babysitter!

Say: *Now you will be asked some questions about the story.*

TEACHER DIRECTIONS:
Read Sample A and the answer choices.

Say: *Now fill in the circle below the correct answer.*

Say: *For Sample B, choose the answer that completes the sentence and makes sense.*

TEACHER DIRECTIONS:
Read Sample B and the answer choices.

Say: *Sample C asks you to use what you learned in the story to decide what might happen the next time Mother Mouse needs to go out.*

TEACHER DIRECTIONS:
Read Sample C and the answer choices.

Say: *Remember to fill in only one circle for each question.*

© McGraw-Hill School Division

Button and Socks

by Kim Valzania

Button liked being a cat, but Socks wanted to be something different.

"It's no fun being a cat," said Socks.

"You are what you are," said Button with a yawn.

Socks went outside and looked around the barnyard.

He saw the pigs rolling in the mud.

"Pigs are too messy. I don't want to be a pig," he thought.

He saw the cows being milked in the barn.

"Cows are too busy. I don't want to be a cow," he thought.

He saw the hens laying eggs.

"Hens are nice. But, I don't know how to lay eggs," he thought.

He saw the dogs herding the sheep.

"Dogs work too hard. I don't want to be a dog," he said.

He saw horses carrying riders on their backs.

"Horses are strong. But I don't want to carry people on my back," he said.

Socks sighed.

He looked over at his friend Button, who was sleeping in a cozy corner of the barn.

"Maybe being a cat isn't so bad after all," he thought.

Socks yawned.

"I am what I am," Socks said to himself.

He walked over to Button, curled up next to him, and took a long nap.

Button and Socks

by Kim Valzania

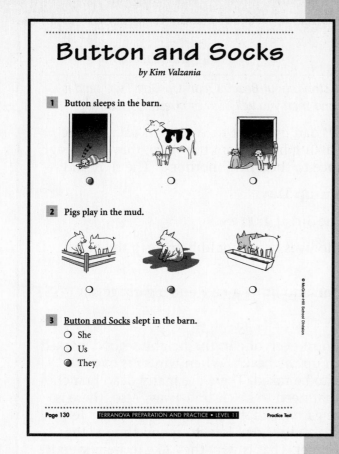

1 Button sleeps in the barn.

     ●   ○   ○

2 Pigs play in the mud.

     ○   ●   ○

3 <u>Button and Socks</u> slept in the barn.
- ○ She
- ○ Us
- ● They

Say: *Find question number 1. Fill in the circle below the picture that best shows what the sentence says.*

Say: *For question number 2, choose the picture that best shows what the sentence says.*

Say: *Now I will read question number 3. Follow along as I read it aloud. Then fill in the circle next to the word that could take the place of the underlined words in the sentence.*

TEACHER DIRECTIONS:
Read question 3 and the answer choices.

Say: *Remembering details from a story is a very important skill. For question number 4, you will have to remember what happens at the end of the story.*

TEACHER DIRECTIONS:
This would be a good time to read the story again. Then read question 4 and the answer choices.

Say: *Find question number 5. Choose the picture that best completes the sentence.*

TEACHER DIRECTIONS:
Read question 5.

Say: *Now try to answer question number 6 without hearing the story again. Fill in the circle below the picture that answers the question.*

4 What happens at the end of the story?
- ○ Socks decides to be a horse.
- ○ Button wakes up when he hears Socks.
- ● Socks sleeps next to Button.

5 Button and Socks are

     ○   ●   ○

6 What kind of animals are the dogs herding in the story?

     ○   ○   ●

STOP

Say: *This is a story about Beach Clean-Up Day. I will read it aloud to you and then you will answer questions 1 through 6.*

Pedro and his dad live next to Whitman Lake. While they were walking home from the store, they saw a sign at the entrance to their neighborhood. The sign said:

Beach Clean-up Day

Saturday, June 3rd at 1:00 P.M.

Everyone who lives here should help keep the beach clean.

Please remember to bring a rake and a garbage bag.

See you there!

Last year, almost everyone in the neighborhood worked hard to clean up the beach. When winter is over, the beach needs to be raked. There are many dead branches and leaves that need to be cleared away. Also, there is usually some garbage that people have carelessly left behind. Pedro and his dad love to spend time at the beach all summer. That is why they like to help keep it clean!

TERRANOVA PREPARATION AND PRACTICE • LEVEL 11

Practice Test

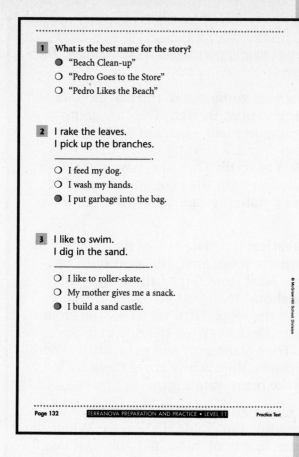

1 What is the best name for the story?
- ● "Beach Clean-up"
- ○ "Pedro Goes to the Store"
- ○ "Pedro Likes the Beach"

2 I rake the leaves.
I pick up the branches.
_____

- ○ I feed my dog.
- ○ I wash my hands.
- ● I put garbage into the bag.

3 I like to swim.
I dig in the sand.
_____

- ○ I like to roller-skate.
- ○ My mother gives me a snack.
- ● I build a sand castle.

Say: *Find question number 1. It asks you to figure out what the whole story is about.*

TEACHER DIRECTIONS:
Read question 1 and the answer choices.

Say: *The next two questions ask you to choose a sentence that finishes a small story. Find question number 2.*

TEACHER DIRECTIONS:
Read question 2 and the answer choices.

Say: *Now find question number 3. Choose the sentence that makes sense after these two sentences.*

TEACHER DIRECTIONS:
Read question 3 and the answer choices.

Say: *Find question number 4. Fill in the circle below the picture that best shows what the sentence says.*

Say: *Find question number 5. Fill in the circle below the picture that best shows what the sentence says.*

Say: *Now read question number 6. Fill in the circle under the picture that best answers the question.*

4 See the sign.

5 Pedro rakes the beach.

6 Which picture shows what Pedro and his dad were doing when they saw the sign?

Say: *Now I will read aloud a story about a class garden. Then you will answer questions 1 through 6.*

James and his class are going out to the playground. They are not going to play, though. They are going to work. They are going to plant a garden. The ground may be muddy, so they are wearing old clothes. They have many packets of seeds. They also have tools. Dan carries the shovel. Bob takes the rake. Dale brings the hoe. Susan carries a watering can. They will need them all.

When the class reaches the place where the garden will be, they put down the tools. First, the grass must be dug up. Digging is hard work. Mrs. Lally will do this job. She uses the shovel to dig up the grass. The children do the rest of the work. First, they rake the ground to make it smooth. Next, they use the hoe to make rows in the soil. They plant corn and pumpkins. When all the seeds are down, they gently cover them with soil. Then they take turns watering.

The seeds will take many months to grow. They will grow all summer while the children are away. When the children return to school in the fall, the corn and pumpkins will be ready. The children will sell them at the school's Fall Fair. They will use the money to buy books for the school library.

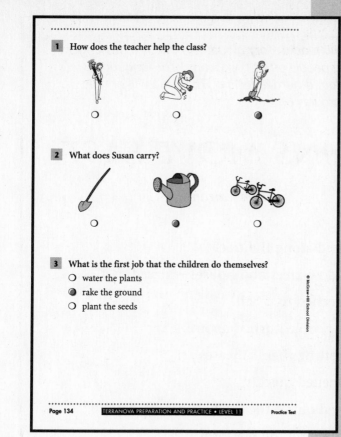

1 How does the teacher help the class?

   ○   ○   ●

2 What does Susan carry?

   ○   ●   ○

3 What is the first job that the children do themselves?
  ○ water the plants
  ● rake the ground
  ○ plant the seeds

© McGraw-Hill School Division

Say: *The next two questions ask you to remember details from the story. After I read each question aloud, fill in the circle under the picture that best answers the question. Find question number 1.*

TEACHER DIRECTIONS:
Read question 1.

Say: *Find question number 2.*

TEACHER DIRECTIONS:
Read question 2.

Say: *Find question number 3.*

TEACHER DIRECTIONS:
Read question 3 and the answer choices.

Say: *Find question number 4.*

TEACHER DIRECTIONS:
Read question 4.

Say: *Question 5 asks you to figure out what the whole story is about.*

TEACHER DIRECTIONS:
Read question 5 and the answer choices.

Say: *Find question 6. Fill in the circle next to the word that can take the place of the underlined word in the sentence.*

TEACHER DIRECTIONS:
Read question 6 and the answer choices.

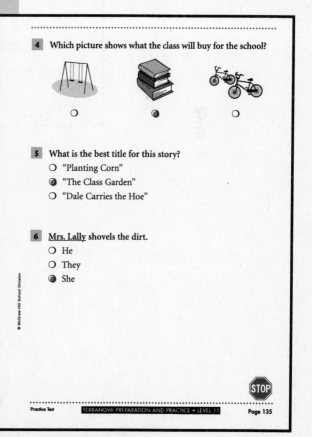

4 Which picture shows what the class will buy for the school?

   ○   ●   ○

5 What is the best title for this story?
  ○ "Planting Corn"
  ● "The Class Garden"
  ○ "Dale Carries the Hoe"

6 <u>Mrs. Lally</u> shovels the dirt.
  ○ He
  ○ They
  ● She

STOP

Say: *Now I will read a story aloud. It is about a passenger train dropping people off at the station. The language is meant to explain a hurried feeling. Then you will answer questions 1 through 6.*

TRAINS MOVE FAST

by Kim Valzania

The train raced along the track.

Out the window, trees and houses whizzed past.

Then, it screeched to a halt.

Quickly, the people hurried about.

They were getting their suitcases.

The doors opened quickly.

People hurried out of the train.

They hurried along the platform.

They didn't want to be late!

The doors slapped shut behind them.

And the train's whistle blew.

Then, it pulled out of the station.

Trains move fast!

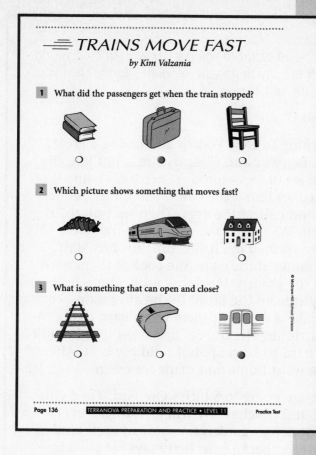

TRAINS MOVE FAST
by Kim Valzania

1 What did the passengers get when the train stopped?

○   ●   ○

2 Which picture shows something that moves fast?

○   ●   ○

3 What is something that can open and close?

○   ○   ●

Say: *Find question number 1. It asks you to remember what happened in the story.*

TEACHER DIRECTIONS:
Read question 1.

Say: *Find question number 2.*

TEACHER DIRECTIONS:
Read question 2.

Say: *Find question number 3. Fill in the circle under the picture that best answers the question.*

TEACHER DIRECTIONS:
Read question 3.

Say: *Find question number 4. This question asks you to figure out why people were doing certain things in the story.*

TEACHER DIRECTIONS:
Read question 4 and the answer choices.

Say: *Find question number 5. Fill in the circle next to the picture that best shows what the sentence says.*

Say: *Find question number 6. Fill in the circle next to the word that has the same vowel sound as rain.*

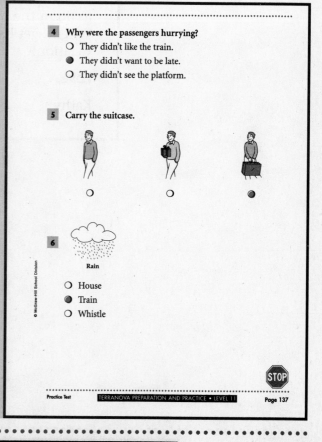

4 Why were the passengers hurrying?
- ○ They didn't like the train.
- ● They didn't want to be late.
- ○ They didn't see the platform.

5 Carry the suitcase.

○   ○   ●

6

Rain

- ○ House
- ● Train
- ○ Whistle

STOP

Say: *Now I will read aloud to you a letter written by a young girl who has left the city to go visit her aunt's farm. Then you will answer questions 1 through 6.*

Dear Mom and Dad,

How is everything in New York? I am having a great time on Aunt Betty's farm. Country life is not like city life. There is a lot of work to do. Yesterday, I helped Aunt Betty feed and milk the cows. Then, I helped feed the chickens and collect the eggs. Then we watered the kitchen garden. We picked the vegetables that were ready. After we washed up, it was time for breakfast. Aunt Betty scrambled the eggs. She cooked them with peppers from the garden. We drank milk. Our whole meal came right from the farm! In the afternoon, we swam in the lake. Last night there was a barn dance. A man played a violin. The dances had steps that I didn't know. It was hard to keep up, but I did my best. After the dance, we went home and made ice cream.

Tomorrow we are going to Smith's Orchard. They grow pears, apples, and peaches. We will give them vegetables from Aunt Betty's garden for some of each kind of fruit. When we get back, Aunt Betty says we need to bake some pies for the County Fair. We are also going to use some of the peaches to make jelly.

I better get to bed now. I'm tired. I have a lot of work to do in the morning. Farm life is fun, but it isn't easy. When I get back, I think I will need a vacation from my vacation!

Love,

Kathy

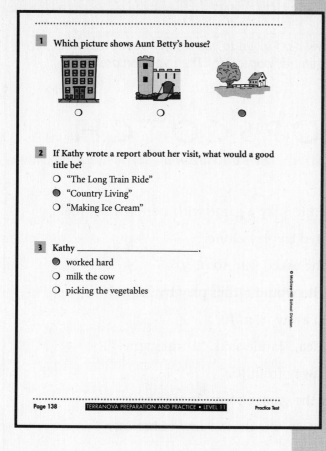

1. Which picture shows Aunt Betty's house?

   ○   ○   ●

2. If Kathy wrote a report about her visit, what would a good title be?
   - ○ "The Long Train Ride"
   - ● "Country Living"
   - ○ "Making Ice Cream"

3. Kathy _____.
   - ● worked hard
   - ○ milk the cow
   - ○ picking the vegetables

© McGraw-Hill School Division

Say: *Find question number 1. It asks you to use what you learned in the story to figure out what Aunt Betty's house looks like.*

TEACHER DIRECTIONS:
   Read question 1.

Say: *Find question number 2. It asks you what the whole story is about.*

TEACHER DIRECTIONS:
   Read question 2 and the answer choices.

Say: *Find question number 3. Fill in the circle next to the words that finishes the sentence correctly and makes sense.*

TEACHER DIRECTIONS:
   Read question 3 and the answer choices.

Say: *Find question number 4. Fill in the circle below the picture that best shows what the sentence says.*

Say: *Find question number 5. Fill in the circle next to the word that has the same sound as cow.*

Say: *Now find question number 6.*

TEACHER DIRECTIONS:
   Read question 6 and the answer choices.

© McGraw-Hill School Division

4. Kathy collects eggs.

   ○   ○   ●

5.

   - ● plow
   - ○ lake
   - ○ tired

6. Which word has the same "a" sound as the word <u>farm</u>?
   - ○ plate
   - ○ apple
   - ● car

STOP

© McGraw-Hill School Division

Say: *Now I will read aloud to you a story about a brother, a sister, and a game of hopscotch. Then you will answer questions 1 through 6.*

HOPSCOTCH

by Kim Valzania

Jamie wanted to play a game with her brother, Joe.

But Joe wanted to play alone.

And when she asked him to play,

Joe told her he would rather play by himself.

Jamie turned away from Joe.

"I have an idea," Jamie said. "A fun game!"

She walked away from Joe.

She went to the garage to get some chalk.

On the driveway, she drew a row of boxes.

She wrote numbers inside them.

She was going to play a game of hopscotch by herself.

Jamie found a small stone.

She tossed it into one of the boxes.

Then she hopped and jumped down the row.

Hopscotch was fun.

Jamie laughed and played by herself.

Joe heard Jamie's laughter.

He wanted to play, too.

He walked over to Jamie.

"I'm sorry about before," he said. "May I play too?"

"Okay," Jamie said. "I would rather play together than play alone."

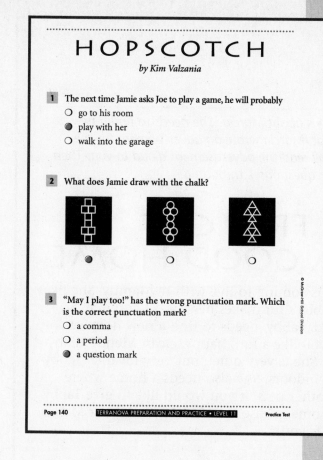

HOPSCOTCH
by Kim Valzania

1 The next time Jamie asks Joe to play a game, he will probably
- ○ go to his room
- ● play with her
- ○ walk into the garage

2 What does Jamie draw with the chalk?

● ○ ○

3 "May I play too!" has the wrong punctuation mark. Which is the correct punctuation mark?
- ○ a comma
- ○ a period
- ● a question mark

© McGraw-Hill School Division

Say: *Find question number 1. It asks you to complete the sentence using what you learned in the story.*

TEACHER DIRECTIONS:
Read question 1 and the answer choices.

Say: *Find question number 2.*

TEACHER DIRECTIONS:
Read question 2.

Say: *Find question number 3. It asks you to fix a punctuation mark.*

TEACHER DIRECTIONS:
Read question 3 and the answer choices.

Say: *Find question number 4. You need to change the sentence into a question. Fill in the circle next to the sentence that is a complete and correct question.*

TEACHER DIRECTIONS:
Read question 4 and the answer choices.

Say: *Find question number 5. It asks you to figure out what the whole story is about.*

TEACHER DIRECTIONS:
Read question 5 and the answer choices.

Say: *Find question number 6. It asks you to remember a detail from the end of the story.*

TEACHER DIRECTIONS:
Read question 6 and the answer choices.

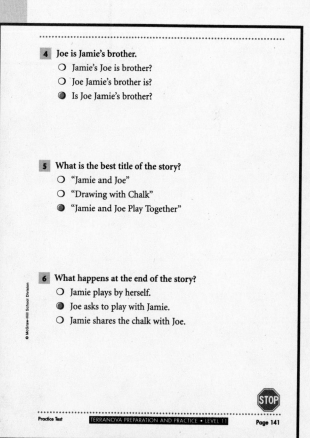

4 Joe is Jamie's brother.
- ○ Jamie's Joe is brother?
- ○ Joe Jamie's brother is?
- ● Is Joe Jamie's brother?

5 What is the best title of the story?
- ○ "Jamie and Joe"
- ○ "Drawing with Chalk"
- ● "Jamie and Joe Play Together"

6 What happens at the end of the story?
- ○ Jamie plays by herself.
- ● Joe asks to play with Jamie.
- ○ Jamie shares the chalk with Joe.

STOP

© McGraw-Hill School Division

FREE CAT TO A GOOD HOME

My grandma is coming to live with my family. She likes Tabby, but Tabby's fur makes her sneeze and itch. So my best friend, Tabby, needs to find a new home. Boo-hoo! Would you like a fun, happy, clean friend? Tabby is a great pet. She is very quiet, but very lovable. Tabby needs to stay indoors. She also needs a home where there are no other pets. If you would like to give Tabby a nice, new home, please call: 652-1258. Ask for Marcia (Tabby's best friend).

© McGraw-Hill School Division

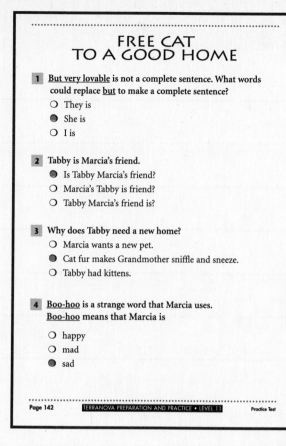

FREE CAT
TO A GOOD HOME

1 <u>But very lovable</u> is not a complete sentence. What words could replace <u>but</u> to make a complete sentence?
- ○ They is
- ● She is
- ○ I is

2 Tabby is Marcia's friend.
- ● Is Tabby Marcia's friend?
- ○ Marcia's Tabby is friend?
- ○ Tabby Marcia's friend is?

3 Why does Tabby need a new home?
- ○ Marcia wants a new pet.
- ● Cat fur makes Grandmother sniffle and sneeze.
- ○ Tabby had kittens.

4 <u>Boo-hoo</u> is a strange word that Marcia uses. <u>Boo-hoo</u> means that Marcia is
- ○ happy
- ○ mad
- ● sad

© McGraw-Hill School Division

Say: *Find question number 1.*

TEACHER DIRECTIONS:
Read question 1 and the answer choices.

Say: *Find question number 2. Find the answer choice that turns the sentence into a complete and correct question.*

TEACHER DIRECTIONS:
Read question 2 and the answer choices.

Say: *Find question number 3. It asks you to remember a detail from the story I just read to you.*

TEACHER DIRECTIONS:
Read question 3 and the answer choices.

Say: *Find question number 4.*

TEACHER DIRECTIONS:
Read question 4 and the answer choices.

Say: *For the next two questions, fill in the circle next to the word that makes the best sense in each blank.*

Say: *Find question number 5. Now listen to this sentence: When Tabby and Marcia went outside, they saw some _____ in the tree.*

TEACHER DIRECTIONS:
Read the answer choices for question 5.

Say: *Find question number 6. Now listen to this sentence: Marcia wanted to _____ some to make a pie.*

TEACHER DIRECTIONS:
Read the answer choices for question 6.

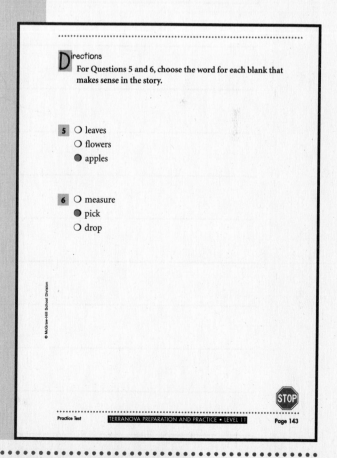

Directions
For Questions 5 and 6, choose the word for each blank that makes sense in the story.

5
- ○ leaves
- ○ flowers
- ● apples

6
- ○ measure
- ● pick
- ○ drop

© McGraw-Hill School Division

STOP

TEACHER NOTES

_____

_____

_____

_____

_____

_____

_____

_____

_____

_____

_____

_____

_____

_____